# you
# need
# this
# book
## to get what
## you want

# you need this book

## to get what you want

Mark Palmer & Scott Solder

SIMON &
SCHUSTER

London · New York · Sydney · Toronto

A CBS COMPANY

First published in Great Britain by Simon & Schuster UK Ltd, 2010
A CBS COMPANY

1 3 5 7 9 10 8 6 4 2

Simon & Schuster UK Ltd
1st Floor
222 Gray's Inn Road
London WC1X 8HB

www.simonandschuster.co.uk

Simon & Schuster Australia
Sydney

A CIP catalogue record for this book is
available from the British Library.

ISBN: 978-1-84737-704-3

Typeset by M Rules
Printed in the UK by CPI Mackays, Chatham ME5 8TD

# Contents

# To start with, here's the end . . .

You might be wondering why we're putting the end of the book at the beginning. It's to give you an idea of what you'll learn and be able to do by the time you've read it. Also it's a way of helping you to remember what you're going to read. Seeing headlines before you get into the detail helps you to absorb information better. So here they are. Just read them through once and carry on.

- Some of what you want is in your own hands. A lot is in the hands of other people. This book is about how you get those things.

- In today's world, getting what you want means constantly adapting your behaviour to fit each situation.

- Thinking is made up of what you see, hear, feel and say to yourself inside your head. To get what you want, you need to ensure the other person is seeing, hearing, feeling and saying to themselves what you want them to.

- You have a specific set of principles, beliefs or values that are different from everyone else's. They are your codes and they determine how you think and behave. One of the best ways of not getting what you want is to assume that other people's codes are the same as yours.

- Getting what you want takes a bit of preparation and thought. Decide exactly what you want before you even begin to go about getting it.

- Everyone has been persuaded before. Most people can be persuaded again. Sometimes they can't be persuaded at all. But then there's always someone else you can persuade if that turns out to be the case.

- The best way to persuade somebody is through their unconscious, or subconscious.

- Sometimes you need to be on the same wavelength as the other person to get what you want. At other times you need to be on different wavelengths.

- To get what you want, you need to work out what the other person wants first.

- Playing the celebrity is the most effective way of getting what you want.

- Getting personal or getting impersonal can get you what you want too, depending on the situation.

- Everyone likes credit. Give people some – but not too much.

- People will often keep their word if you make them feel they owe you.

- The words you choose, and the way you say them, can persuade people without them realizing.

- Be ready for your enemies and be prepared to stop them getting what they want.

# Why you need this book to get what you want

This book is the most effective way to get you what you want in a very modern world. Think about all the things you want today. Some of them are in your own hands, and many of them are in the hands of others. This book is about thinking and communicating differently so you can get both.

Of course it would be so much better if you could get other people on your side instantly, wouldn't it. You probably know that when people relate to you and like you, you are more likely to relate to them and like them back. Yes – sometimes that basic transaction does get you what you want. But it's not just about that. Not any more. Times have changed.

Winning friends to influence people has worked well up to now – but you've probably seen that it doesn't always work the way it used to. People don't seem to play by the rules any more. Actually, they do – but it's a new set of rules. There's a new world order. You need to know what it is, but more importantly you need to know how to work within it. The fact that you're holding this book now means you must be serious about getting what you want. And I'm talking about the sorts of things that are really important – at home, at work, with your friends . . . and with your enemies.

You need this book to get:

- the job you want

- your partner to give a damn

- your boss on side

- the love life you need

- the pay rise you deserve

- what you want from a meeting

- a real work/life balance

- a refund at the shops

- out of a parking fine

- the kids dressed and ready for school on time

- served at the bar when it's busy

- more than you've already got

. . . the list goes on.

## What makes this book unique

Once you've absorbed what this book says, it will be hard to forget it. You can use it for almost any situation that requires dealing with other people. Of course, there will be times when nothing's going to work and you just have to walk away. But not many.

You will absorb most of the big and juicy stuff at an unconscious level. No memory required. Well, maybe just a bit.

This book works on two different levels, so you learn twice. First, you read the book at face value to learn how to use it to get what you want – from yourself and from other people.

Second, once you've read through it, you'll be nicely set up for the 'You need this book unmasked' section at the end. This will explain the psychological techniques used throughout the book to help you absorb information like a sponge, so it's really hard to forget. Once you're aware of the techniques we've used, you'll be able to cherry-pick the ones that you would like to add to what you already know. Imagine you're watching a magic show with a difference; at the end of this show you'll have the chance to learn all the secrets of being a magician. Don't go there yet, though. It really won't make any sense at the moment. In fact, this is a good time to tell you that it's best to read this book in the right order. The first chapters – the ones before we get to the persuasion techniques – are there to lay the foundations in your mind so you begin thinking in a different way. If I used jargon, I'd say the first part of the book was there to give you new strategies in the way that you think.

## What you get

Unlike other books, this one helps you to retain a lot of what you learn unconsciously. In other words, you won't have to try too hard to remember what you read. You'll absorb it easily just by taking your time, reading it through and practising the techniques as they come up. If you do this, you'll find you just seem to 'get it'. The learning processes are like those that you used when learning to walk, talk, ride a bike or drive a car. Once you've mastered them, you'll find it hard to forget them.

## What does this book do?

It's a formula, a template, a recipe, a simple process to get what you want. That means thinking in different ways to understand yourself better, achieve more and get more from your life. And you'll learn techniques to persuade other people so you can get what you want from them too.

By the way, this is probably a good time to clear something up. Some people might call this 'manipulation'. The truth is that people only use that word when the outcome is in some way sinister. When it's not, the word magically becomes 'influencing' or 'persuading'. Life is all about getting other people to do things that work for you, and vice versa. That's what society's all about. That's how humans evolved and that's why you're alive today and reading this book. It's just about being successful. Deciding what you want and then going out and getting it is the key to being successful.

There's also a simple memory technique at the end of the

book to reinforce it all. All you need to know for now is that everything you will read is relevant and specifically designed to enable you to solve problems, come up with solutions and get you what you really want.

## Here's how it works . . .

There are two of us writing this. Mark and Scott. You might want to bear this in mind as you read, but you'll notice that very often we won't tell you who's saying what. There's a reason for that, a good reason. It's one of the ways that we have of helping you to remember what you read without trying too hard. The two of us will help you remember the important things as you go. Even when it's not immediately obvious why we're telling you a particular story, there's always a good reason for you to read it. So when you read about pond life, lost hamsters, T-shirts, visits to the loo in the middle of the night and other apparently random stories, bear with us. It's all relevant. They're there to help you to start thinking differently.

At times, reading this book you might feel a little confused. You may even notice that things go off on the odd tangent. Or some sentences will seem to stop abruptly. That's all deliberate. Think of it as a helping hand to speed up your memory processes without you really having to try. If you do feel confused at times, that's OK. It'll only last for a short time and things will start to make sense again almost instantly. There are two of us contributing to this book and this is going to help you. You'll also find that some of the techniques are given in two different ways, and this will help your memory and learning processes.

Of course, feeling confused can be a good thing. When you're confused, it means your brain is working overtime to make sense of something. And confusion is usually a sign that you're about to learn something new. Think back to the first day in your current job. You didn't know who to speak to, where to go or what to do. It was highly confusing. Then, things got a bit clearer. Suddenly, things became second nature. What do you think was going on in your brain to get from 'highly confusing' to 'second nature'? The sensation of being confused is your brain's way of telling the subconscious part of it (the part that does most of the work) that it needs answers. That's why, when you're confused, you often get 'brainwaves' that apparently come from nowhere. What's really happening is that you're not confused at all. The conscious part of your brain may feel confused, but the subconscious part is busy processing everything it knows to get you the answers. And it's doing it at about a million miles an hour. That's too much and too fast for the conscious part, which is why it can't keep up. So never fear. The next time you feel confused by something, relax! It means your subconscious brain is busy working it out. Confusion leads to learning.

A lot of people who have experienced our live seminars have asked us to write this book. I hesitated for quite a while, because I couldn't work out how to convey all of the live techniques. One of the techniques to help people retain information is to go off on tangents. Tangents help us learn because they're a great way of grabbing and keeping people's attention. You rarely drift off when someone goes off on a tangent, do you? You actually hang on to every word, wondering when the speaker will get back to the point. Which means you can't drift off. Still with me? So, at times when you find me going off on a tangent, you'll also find that the tangent contains a key message that's good for you to retain. The fact that I deliver it via a tangent is one of the ways to help you remember stuff without really trying. I'll also make sure I tell you the point of each tangent at the end.

So here's the first tangent. I'm pointing this one out in advance so you're ready for it. But in future the tangents will be unannounced as they work better that way. You'll learn more about how to use this technique yourself, when we talk about the 'meeting before the meeting' later.

That reminds me. The other day someone on television was talking about procrastination. He said being a procrastinator is like living your life in a fog. You can't enjoy anything because you've always got at least one thing hanging over you that you should be doing instead. It's much better to just get on with things so they don't hang over you. True. But not very helpful. If you could, you would, wouldn't you? How is it that those who procrastinate begin to do so as soon as there's something to do? The fact that you can procrastinate straight away means you have the ability to do *something* straight away. That something can be the thing you want to do. It can be getting out of bed on time, doing the washing up, finally dumping him or her, finishing that report, filling in your tax return, paying the bills, changing your job or anything you keep putting off.

So the point of that tangent was this: if you can procrastinate straight away, then you do know how to do something straight away. All you need to do is apply that to other things –

not just procrastination. That's a really good way to look at it if you're a procrastinator. The best way to do something you keep putting off is to do the first thing. Nothing more. Just make a start. That means just opening a new email and writing in the subject box, simply getting the lawnmower out of the shed or just dealing with the first thing in that pile of paperwork. You'll usually find you end up finishing the whole job reasonably easily.

So now I've got that tangent out of the way, where was I? I was talking about how we translated our live seminars into this book. I was having difficulty working out how to do it, until my weak bladder rescued me. On one of my many trips to the loo in the middle of the night, I had a 'eureka' moment and came up with the answer. I realized we needed to write this book in this way. We are imagining that you are a member of a live audience and we are talking to you the way we would to them. That means you are now reading the book, following the words, and seeing a few things in your mind's eye (especially at the mention of the live audience). And if you weren't seeing pictures in your mind's eye before, you certainly are now, aren't you?

Making the right pictures in your head can be very useful. Although the wrong pictures can be unhelpful, especially if you let them run riot. However, it's too soon to go into more detail on that.

So, how are you? Good? Not so good? Don't know? Something else? There's a reason you've decided to read this book now. You must know at least one person who isn't playing ball at the moment. And that person could even be you. No doubt you've tried your usual tactics but so far nothing has worked. Before we get going, there are some important bits about you that we need to introduce first. (You'll love the next few pages because they're all about YOU.)

# 1

# How You Got to Where You Are

Right, we need to talk about your parents having sex. Sorry, we know it's not nice but keep reading and that'll take your mind off those pictures in your head that you don't want to be there.

Anyway, back to your mum and dad. Wherever they were and whatever position they were in (sorry – couldn't resist!) when they conceived you, the fact is that their simple, instinctive urge to do it ended up bringing you into the world. The same goes for your grandparents, great-grandparents and so on – all the way back to before we were even human.

## Remember This
*To get a proper idea of what you need to do now to be successful and get what you want, you need to know what humans have done already to be so successful so far. That's all you need to remember for now. Don't worry about why. It's coming.*

Humans have been successfully creating new humans for millions of years. Your ancestors before that were ape-like creatures successfully creating new ape-like creatures. In fact, as you probably know, if you look back far enough, you'll discover that your great-great-great- (add thousands of 'greats' here) grandfather was a bacteria swimming around in a pool of soup with all his bacteria mates, all frantically dividing themselves into duplicates as fast as possible in a race to see who could be first to become an amoeba.

And just when those new amoebas thought they could have a rest – no. A new race was on to see who could be first to become a sponge. Some didn't take part in that race and became mushrooms instead. For some of those new sponges there was no let up. Eventually some of them ended up as primates and they ended up ruling the world. Meanwhile, some of the sponges had been doing it a different way and ended up as dinosaurs, birds and all kinds of other animals. Some sponges didn't bother with any of it and just ended up in the bathrooms of some primates and were used to scrub their backs. By the way, if you've got a sponge in your bathroom you should be ashamed of yourself. That's no way to treat your distant cousin.

> **ALERT! *How to achieve exactly the opposite of what this book is intended to achieve* –**
>
> Dig in your heels, refuse to change, do everything the way you've always done it, whatever is going on around you, even though it's not working as well as it used to.

This is not only true for an evolving species. It's also true in all walks of life. Adapting to change when it comes along means you'll do well.

Someone I know hasn't changed for a long time. Not since he was at school. When he was at school he realized that a certain way of behaving got him what he wanted. It worked well so he kept on doing it. He was a boy of few words, and it was the sort of school where actions spoke loudest anyway. By saying little, apart from the odd, clever and well-chosen sarcastic comment, he shot to the top. He became popular and well respected. You might wonder why being quiet and sarcastic won him respect. The answer is that I don't know. The point is, it doesn't matter. All I know – and all he knew at the time – was that it worked for him then. The problem is that now, years after he hung up his school uniform, he's still doing the same thing. But it doesn't work any more. Now he's an adult, people just think he's rude, insensitive and a bit of a . . . you know what I mean?

That tangent was about this: just because something was successful before doesn't necessarily mean it will always be successful. So if your behaviour stops working for you, then you need to change the way you behave. The trick is to notice when it stops working. Many people don't realize that what they do in certain situations has stopped working.

From time to time in this book, we'll be asking you to 'Do This'. Whenever a 'Do This' comes along, it's important that you take your time and do it because it gets you thinking in a different way. And that means you're becoming more adaptable. Here's the first one.

**DO THIS**

- Pick something you want – that you have been trying to get for some time – but you are not getting. That could be a job, a partner, a pay rise, a new waistline, anything you like.

- Jot down a list of what you have been doing until now to get it.

- Look at the list you have written down. Cross off anything that you have tried more than three times but has not worked. (Even if it used to work for you in the past.)

- Once you have crossed them off, not before, do 'the next step'.

- What else can you do that you haven't tried yet? Add it to the list.

Back to evolution. Look down at your feet. How did you learn to stand on two legs? How do you think your toes shrank down into those phalanges at the end of each foot, to enable you to stand up straight rather than hold on to branches of trees while swinging through them? You advanced primate, you. How did you pull that off? And, going back all those millions of years, how did that great ancestor of yours, the amoeba, manage to change and evolve?

While you're soaking all that up, I'll explain what I've been talking about in a different way. I'm talking about success stories. What makes some people – and some species – so successful, while others are not?

What have Madonna, George Michael, Kylie Minogue, Elton John and Tom Jones got in common? They're all pop stars, yes.

But not that. They're all successful pop stars. More than that, they're icons. More than that, they've been successful for years. And years. Has any one of them stayed the same? If you were asked to describe any of their acts, what would you say? You can't describe them. Because it depends on when I'm talking about, doesn't it? Each one of these acts is successful because it has changed and adapted.

What's the difference between the universe, space, the heavens, the galaxy and the sky? In English, aren't they roughly the same thing? Or are they in English at all? No they're not, they're Greek, Latin, German and Norse. That's why the English language has done so well around the world. It hasn't resisted change (in this case, the influence of foreign words). Quite the opposite; English has welcomed them in and adopted them as its own. How has English managed to establish itself as the international language? It's responded to changes by changing itself.

I know part of you is now getting the picture. But there's another part of you that hasn't fully tuned in yet. Change, where necessary, means success. Change for the sake of change doesn't. Being adaptable equals success. The most successful people and systems have adapted to changing times, trends, needs and demands. Relatively quickly. Think about the last time a shop or store near you went bust. Sometimes it's just bad luck. Usually, though, it's because it didn't respond quickly enough to the changing needs of the market.

Here's what happened to a friend of mine, Mark, who didn't adapt quickly enough in his job when things changed around him. Believe me, he's no Madonna. He's changed a lot since he joined the army, nearly unrecognizable. These days he sports a massive brown moustache. Perhaps that means he's grown up. Before he joined the army he had the life of Riley, a laid-back sort of bloke. In summer, even at work, he would don aqua-blue surfing shorts and neon-yellow flip flops. In the office he'd sit with his perma-tanned orange feet up on the desk watching cricket. The only time he got out of his seat was to walk into the kitchen to help himself to the free bottles of mineral water that his employers supplied to all staff. Very generous. Four hundred staff helped themselves to endless bottles of crystal-clear blue water, delivered daily by two very fit people from the post room. I'm not sure how successful that company was in the end, but I'd say it probably isn't around now.

Mark drank a lot of water. And in the evenings, he drank a lot too. For him, life was one big party. He could do what he wanted, when he wanted, how he wanted, with the people he wanted at home and at work. He knew how to get what he wanted. At the time.

Recessions come and recessions go, and one day one came. The never-ending mineral water dried up. The televisions disappeared from the office. Mark and his colleagues weren't even allowed to listen to the radio. Breakfast meetings went ahead – but with no breakfast. 'Beer' Friday suddenly became 'Get your head down and get on with your work or you'll be fired Friday'. 'Working from home today' became 'I don't care if you've got a hangover, get your backside into work now'. 'I'm off for a client lunch, see you tomorrow', became 'Be back at your desk by two. And if you're hungry, grab a sandwich from the supermarket on your way back'.

The chummy atmosphere between managers and staff also dried up. No more Tellytubby-style nicknames for the most senior people – like Dipsy, Flopsy, La-la, Smythie and Donny (I am serious, here. It really was like this, according to Mark). For the more veteran senior managers, the status title of 'Uncle' was replaced by what you and I might call the more conventional style of 'Mr'. Large voluptuous leather sofas – the badges of honour for bosses with their own offices who wanted to bask in their own seniority – were replaced by a regular roasting about profits, losses and performance. There were no more quarterly target reports. They were replaced with 'How much money have you made this company today?' The Tellytubby mask slipped to reveal the face of the dark side. Conversations about performance took place in corridors rather than in meeting rooms. And if he or she thought you weren't giving him or her your fullest attention he or she would cut you down with the words 'Am I boring you, sonny?' And the bigger the audience there was when that happened, the better.

Mark and his closest friends didn't last long. They were made redundant. They weren't really enjoying their jobs anyway, so it didn't matter much at first. They thought they'd just find more work, more mineral water, more beer and more mates somewhere else. They didn't. Times were tough – and in recession.

Look at how Mark approached life – and how he got on. He was doing fine, breezing through life at work, putting his suntanned feet up and generally chilling out in the office when his company was happy for him to do that. More to the point, his company had *encouraged* that sort of behaviour at the time because it was proud of its laid-back, friendly culture. When that changed, what did he do? The same as before. He carried on chilling out, putting his feet up, calling his bosses silly but affectionate nicknames and all the rest of it. He didn't adapt when things began to change. And where did he end up? Out the door. Now compare that with the human race, Madonna and the English language. Poles apart.

I don't know much Polish but I know more than I did six months ago. I'm learning it because my girlfriend is Polish and her parents don't speak English. There's only so much pointing, talking slowly in English and playing charades that you can do before you get fed up with it.

Here's what I know so far:

dzień dobry

dziękuję

and

nawet nie chcę myśleć o tym, że moi rodzice uprawiają sex (I don't like thinking of my parents having sex)

Ask Charles Darwin. He told us centuries ago that being adaptable leads to success. The reason why a particular animal (that's you) rules the world is that humans have adapted *whenever they have needed to.* Unlike their long lost and long deceased cousins, *Homo habilis, Homo neanderthalis* and *Homo australis.*

## Conclusion

Obviously, you haven't got millions of years to adapt slowly and be successful. The good news is you don't need that long. Now that you know the principle, you can apply it in your everyday life. If something changes, and what you're doing suddenly isn't working any more, then the quicker you can change it and do something else instead, the sooner you'll be successful. That could happen in a matter of days, hours, minutes or even just a few seconds. And only having one way (and sticking to it) of doing things will severely limit your chances of getting what you want.

# 2

# How Adaptable Are You?

Having read the last chapter, you might be thinking to yourself, 'Yes, I get all that but I'm pretty adaptable already.' That may be true, but there are probably areas in your life where you do the same thing a lot. Everyone has routines. Routines are there to make your life simpler. Some of them are really good and useful but if you have too many, or you leave them in place for too long, you end up not exercising the part of your brain controlling your adaptability. And like a muscle, if you don't use it – it gets weaker. And the more you use it, the better it gets.

So, it's true to say this for everybody: there's always room to be more adaptable. This chapter is about exercising your adaptability muscle so being more adaptable becomes second nature. By being more flexible about the smaller, everyday stuff, you'll develop your adaptability about the bigger stuff that crops up less frequently. I mean things like getting a new relationship, a pay rise, dealing with problem people and – well – getting what you want in general.

Let's start by finding out where you have routines.

**DO THIS**

Answer these questions. We'll come to the answers in a second.

- How do you get to work?

- What do you order when you go to your favourite restaurant?

- Where do you go on holiday?

- What do you do on Friday nights?

- What time do you go to bed?

- Which magazines do you read?

- Which perfume or aftershave do you wear?

- What is the first thing you do when you get up in the morning?

It's probable that you could answer most – or all – of those questions. That means, like all of us, you have routines. More than you thought. You probably go to work the same way, you may well go to the same place on holiday, you almost definitely follow the same routine each time you get out of bed in the morning, and do many other things the same way. We all do.

The thing about humans (or slightly advanced non-mushroom primates, as I prefer to call them) is that we think we're original, adaptable, and love trying different things. We want to think we're unpredictable. In fact, we love to think we're *so* unpredictable, that it's all rather predictable.

Don't believe me? Then do this.

Ever played 'rock, paper, scissors'?

## Rock, paper, scissors

OK, here we go. Best of five.

Count to three and then throw. My throw is on the following page – no cheating!

As you play, feel free to refer back to our previous throws – it might help.

**Round 1**

1, 2, 3

Throw! (now turn the page to see my throw)

I threw paper

## Round 2

Ready?

1, 2, 3

Throw! (now turn the page to see my throw)

I threw scissors. I at least got a draw, right?

## Round 3

1, 2, 3

Throw! (now turn the page to see my throw)

Damn I threw the scissors again. What are the chances? You threw paper, right?

## Round 4

1, 2, 3

Throw! (turn the page to see my throw)

I threw scissors again . . . so predictable.

One last go. This game is hard, isn't it? You've got to do better this time round to put in a solid performance. Ready? Make a firm choice this time.

## Round 5

1, 2, 3

Throw! (now turn the page to see my throw)

I threw paper!

I win, you just didn't make the cut this time. I had the game all wrapped up.

I don't claim to have second-guessed you every time. We would need to be face to face for that. And I said people are predictable – not boring! But, if you played me at 'rock, paper scissors', how well did I do?

However adaptable people are, they still have patterns of behaviour to some degree. The key is to be aware of as many as you can, so you can change them from time to time.

To get you started, we've done a few things in this book differently from how you would expect them to be. That means you're going to have to read certain bits in a way that you don't usually.

This is how you start building your adaptability muscle, so you can make a habit of adapting quickly and painlessly when you need to. The more you do things differently for the sake of it, the easier you'll find your adaptability muscle responds to change. And change will come. It always does. Adapting to change gets you what you want.

## Conclusion

Get more adaptable by making a point of doing things differently. Go to work a different way, eat different foods at different times and make your tea or coffee at a different point in your morning routine whenever you can. You can go to other places on holiday with other people. You can do something different this weekend. Think of something you usually do and now do something else. Even if it's just the once. You can do something different from now, for ever, at least once a week.

# 3

# Know Your Thinking

## What you say to yourself

Some people call it your internal dialogue. Sometimes it's called the voice in your head. It's the same thing – it's what you say to yourself when you're thinking about stuff. Your internal dialogue has a direct impact on the way you think and behave. Letting it run wild and out of control is never a good thing. Whatever your internal dialogue is saying can have a serious effect on your mood and your frame of mind.

For all kinds of reasons, this used to be one of my favourite sayings – 'What's the point?'

I'd say it all the time to myself, whenever things got a bit difficult. It goes without saying what effect that had on me and on other people. And how adaptable do you think I was, if that was all I'd say whenever something turned out to be a bit of a challenge?

Let's try out your internal dialogue. Think of someone you don't get on with. Someone you don't like, who's so different from you that it's not just a clash, it's a head-on collision. You can't understand where they're coming from and they don't get you either. As soon as I mentioned that person, your internal dialogue will have probably gone off the scale. In other words, that voice in your head started chattering away at you like it always does, going on about this person and how wrong they are.

Sometimes you say good things to yourself, and other times you come out with a load of unhelpful stuff. You tell yourself when you think you can't do something and you tell yourself when you're not looking forward to something and you keep on delivering similar messages to yourself in lots of different ways to make sure you really listen. Stop reading for a second. No stop! What are you saying to yourself at the moment? Don't read on until you can answer this question. People do differ in how much they talk to themselves in their head, but everyone does it to some extent. (By the way, if you're a fast reader, it usually means you don't talk to yourself as much as other people do. That wasn't really a tangent – just an interesting, but completely irrelevant, piece of information.)

OK, now read on. It's not all bad, though. At times, you tell yourself really good stuff too. You tell yourself when something is going well, and when you're looking forward to something. Have you ever noticed that when you tell yourself good things, they usually come true? And obviously, when you tell yourself bad things, they usually come true too. Like the times when you've said to yourself 'Oh God, I'm having a bad day' – and the day just got worse and worse.

So, I'm guessing you'd really like to learn how to get

that voice to work for you, rather than against you. That means getting it to say good stuff rather than bad stuff. Easy. Don't just take our word for it. Remember Michael Phelps in the 2008 Olympics? Was he saying to himself in a weedy, whining nasal voice, 'I don't think I'm going to win this? These Speedos are so tight, they're killing me. My sex life's over for at least a week.'? No, Michael is in control of his internal dialogue. He makes sure it says the right things at the right times.

Here's an example of someone who doesn't control their internal dialogue quite so well. A few years ago Lisa always used to moan about how much she hated her job. For 'no reason in particular', she really hated her boss and went around saying how much she disliked being at work. How can you not like somebody for 'no reason in particular'? Everything everyone does is for a reason, whether they're aware of the reason or not. She *said* she had no reason – that's all. And she probably *thought* she had no reason too. Anyway, the more she said she hated her boss, the more she wound herself up and reinforced what she was saying in her mind. What was she doing? Without knowing it, she was talking herself into hating her boss and her job even more. A great example of using your internal voice against yourself.

Lisa began waking up every morning telling herself how much she hated her boss. In the hour between waking up and arriving at work, she'd managed to convince herself she was going to have a bad day and that she would hate her job today even more than she'd hated it yesterday. Soon, she began to feel sick every time she got into her car to go to work. Then she felt sick when she got into her car, whether she was going to work or not. One day she had to pull over and throw up on the side of the road. She then sold her car because getting into it made her feel ill.

Your internal dialogue is a persuasive thing. Most people don't realize they have an internal dialogue, let alone an internal dialogue that could do with some improvement. It's only when you stop and take the time to ask 'What am I saying to myself?' that you begin to tune into your own frame of mind. Once you do that, it's really easy to replace negative internal dialogue with a better one.

How many times in your life does your internal dialogue kick off in a negative way? I'll ask you this question now: does that ever help you get what you want? The answer is no. Never.

---

**DO THIS**

Tune into your internal dialogue.

Choose a point in your daily routine when you always, or almost always, manage to grab some time entirely to yourself. Even if it's just for a couple of minutes. The best time for this is in the morning when you wake up. If that's not convenient, then you can choose other moments: in the bathroom, on the way to or from work, at bedtime, waiting for someone or something, or any moment that is in any way 'downtime' for you.

Once you've got your moment, get yourself a pen and paper and jot down what your internal dialogue has been saying up until now. In fact, what's it saying as you write? Jot down absolutely anything, however irrelevant or trivial it may seem. It could even be a song. Jot that down too – who knows what your unconscious is trying to tell you? Unless you've just heard the song on the radio, there's probably a reason why you're singing it to yourself. Write down the lyrics. What do they say?

Anything and everything has an unconscious reason for being there. Keep what you've got written down. Go back to it twenty-four hours later. If you can, do it every day for as long as a week to get a full idea of your internal dialogue.

Now look at what you've written down. Is it helping you or not? If it's not – begin saying something else to yourself, something more useful. Think of something you're looking forward to, and say to yourself how much you're looking forward to it. Or think of something that makes you happy, and say to yourself how happy it makes you. You'll feel different in minutes.

And keep saying that until it's a good new habit.

Your internal dialogue can work against you or for you. If you find that you say negative things about yourself to yourself or other people, then it's good to change that. The best way to take note of what you're saying to yourself is to take time out and write it down. Change anything negative into something positive and start saying that to yourself instead. Before long, you'll be thinking more positively automatically.

## What you see

Thinking is a complex business. As well as your internal dialogue, you also have internal pictures. Both of these create feelings and emotions, so it's important to have the right internal dialogue and the right pictures.

Have you heard of someone called Tom Brady? You may not have heard of him because he's an American footballer. He's the David Beckham of American football and he knows how to make his internal pictures work for him. When he practises, he imagines he's playing a real game. In his mind he sees the stadium, the crowd, his team-mates, the opposition and he makes sure he hears them too.

Does Tom take hallucinogenic drugs? No. Does he have a Hollywood set designer on hand to mock up the real game for him? No. He just makes his own pictures in his head so that the practice game seems like the real game. And Tom Brady is a three times Superbowl winner, two times Superbowl MVP, holder of the National Football League record for the most touchdown passes in a single season, *Sports Illustrated* Sportsman of the Year – and part of the team that recorded the longest consecutive winning streak in NFL history. He also won Male Athlete of the Year – the first NFL player to take the title since Joe Montana. That's what making good pictures in your head can get you.

Now it's your turn. For now, I'm going to choose your subject for you but you'll soon be able to choose your own. I'm going to use flying.

Ever been on a plane in turbulence? You know when it

suddenly drops like a stone? You can feel your stomach in your throat. You're tossed around in mid-air, and you find yourself grabbing the armrests with white knuckles. Like you, the other passengers are trying to look like they're not bothered. But they are really. In fact, you're all going 'aaarrrggghhh' in your heads. Maybe you've suddenly found God. Think back to when you were last frightened. What pictures did you have in your mind's eye when you were frightened? What did you see? Here's what I see when this happens to me. It might not be the same as yours, but you'll get the picture. I see a crash site with smouldering plumes of smoke. Carnage. The plane is ripped in half and there's a search and rescue crew going through it. They find my charred passport but no sign of me. OK, I'm no great fan of flying but there was a time when I couldn't even get on the plane because of those pictures I kept making. However mild or serious your pictures are, you can just change them like I did to make them better.

Before I knew any of what you're reading about now, I tried to tell myself not to think about the plane crashing. I tried not to think about the flames, the smoke, the charred passport and all the rest of it. But the more I tried not to think about it, the more I found myself thinking about it. That happens when you try not to think about things. Once I knew how to do it properly – it worked. The trick is this: don't do what most other people do and try *not* to think about it. Just change *how* you're thinking about it. To get over it, I learned a technique which works really well for anything that you find frightening. This is what I did:

- I thought of the whole crash scene as usual – with smoke, the charred passport, the wreckage, the flames and everything else, but I removed the colour and made it a black and white picture. It's easy because I've seen black and white films on TV, so I know what black and white scenes look like.

- I imagined I was watching it in the cinema – and it was playing on the screen some distance away from me. I would be sitting near the back row.

- I imagined myself shrinking the cinema screen to half its size.

- I repeated that process again and again whenever I thought of flying. Now I do it automatically.

Now when I fly, I hardly get scared at all. So much so, that I can't really remember what it felt like to be terrified of flying. If you're scared of flying – do the same. Whatever pictures and sounds come to mind when you think of flying, just make them less real – don't try to change what's in them. Of course, you can do it for any fear – it doesn't have to be flying.

Who do you think this is, talking about his bad pictures?

'The din from the crowd was overwhelming. *I was like a rabbit caught in the headlights.* At that moment I wanted to be anywhere else but on the track. My nerves would get the better of me before every race, especially if my family and friends were watching.'

Those are the words of the British triple Olympic gold medal winner, world record holder, BBC Sports Personality of the Year, he of the massive thighs and tight Lycra shorts, Sir Chris Hoy, before he learned how to change his pictures. That's how powerful this is. He used it to win gold medals, and you can use it too. You can overcome fears, build your own confidence, deal with things you're dreading and even change bad memories. All you do is make the good stuff more real in your mind and the bad stuff less real by changing certain aspects of how you think about it. And here's the important bit: once you've got your own pictures and sounds right, you'll be able to create the right pictures and sounds in other people's minds so you can persuade them. And that means you'll get what you want. But that bit comes later.

## DO THIS

Read through this fully first before you do it. What are you not looking forward to at the moment, but you know you're going to have to do anyway at some point? It can be anything at all. Wait. Don't read on until you've thought of it. It might be going to the dentist, having a difficult conversation at work, dumping someone, going to work on Monday morning, or anything else. Got it? Freeze.

Now you've got it. As you think about that now, notice the picture you make in your head. Now, do the following things in turn and make a mental note of which one makes you feel better about the thing you have to do. One technique may work better than the other. If so, which one is it?

- Imagine you've flicked a switch and the picture has suddenly gone black and white.

- Take hold of the picture in your mind and throw it into the distance so it's further away from you but you can still see it – as if it's on a cinema screen.

- Shrink the cinema screen to half its size. And, just for fun, shrink it again.

How differently do you feel now? Not so bad after all, is it? And all you did was change the way you saw the pictures. Before you read on, take a moment now and do what you just did, but do it again. Once you've done it a couple of times and really noticed the difference, have a think about something else you're not looking forward to and do the same. Take your time. There's no rush. The rest of the book will still be here when you come back.

OK, so now you've got that bit. Read on.

## Do the two of you want the same thing?

You know about your internal dialogue and your pictures and how you can control them to change the way you feel. If you've read books on the power of the unconscious mind, you'll be familiar with some of what you're about to read.

I mentioned before that we make a lot of our points in two different ways. We say things twice because there are two of you. Two parts of you, in fact. Allow me – and me – to introduce you . . . to you. You've both met before and you know each other intimately. It helps if you like each other, but that's not always the case. You've been known to bicker in the past. And then the sparks really fly. If you're serious about getting what you want, you need to make sure that the two parts of you are going after the same thing. If they're not, you'll find yourself in two minds. Literally.

Before you read on, think about something you're in two minds about. Something you've been meaning to do, but for some reason you haven't done. Something you have a slight doubt about, even though you don't really know why.

I remember when I was in two minds, aged thirteen. I was young, teenage and slightly spotty. I had a girlfriend. Her name was – let's call her Siobhan. I'd been going out with Siobhan for a few weeks (a long time when you're thirteen) but I had a problem. I wasn't sure whether or not to carry on going out with her. So being a pragmatic type (albeit still slightly spotty) I thought the best way to decide was to draw up a list of pros and cons about Siobhan.

If I were talking to you as part of a live audience, I would usually take cover at this point or duck. People have been known to chuck things in my direction when I confess this.

So I started with the pros. I must have come up with six or seven reasons (good reasons, I thought), to stay with her.

Then I moved over to the cons. And I could only find one reason not to go out with her.

I dumped her. Sorry, Siobhan, if you're reading.

Once both parts of me were in agreement again, I felt a lot better even if Siobhan didn't.

What's this all about then? The two parts of you are your conscious and your unconscious. Some people also call it your subconscious. It doesn't really matter. You're usually conscious of the conscious part of your brain. Everything that you're aware of at this moment is being processed by the conscious part of your brain. For example, you're aware of holding this book and reading the words on this page, as well as other things around you.

Everything else is being run by the unconscious part. For example, your breathing, your blinking, your digestion, or something in the back of your mind that you know you are good at.

Actually, things pop between your consciousness and unconsciousness all the time. Just like they did just now. Your breathing, your blinking and your digestion popped briefly into your conscious awareness when I mentioned them. So did the thing you're good at. They're still there because I'm still mentioning them. But very soon, they'll sink back into your unconsciousness because you don't need to think consciously about them all the time. Breathing is actually harder when you think about it consciously, isn't it? In fact, it's far easier to allow your breathing autopilot to take care of your breathing, your blinking autopilot to take care of your blinking and your making-a-cup-of-coffee-in-the-morning autopilot to take care of how you do that. An autopilot is a piece of automatic behaviour, pure and simple. There's a whole section on this coming up soon.

The point here is that my unconscious brain knew all along that I didn't want to go out with Siobhan any more. The fact that I made a list of pros and cons *at all* tells you everything. Why would I have done that if my unconscious had thought everything was fine?

To put it another way, even though I had more conscious pros than unconscious cons, deep down in my heart I knew what I really wanted. Head versus heart. You've probably heard of that before. I prefer to call it the conscious and unconscious.

---

### DO THIS

- What do you know deep down at the moment that you're trying to ignore? You'll know you're ignoring it because you'll be saying things to yourself like 'I'm confused', 'I don't know what to do', 'I can't decide', 'Something's bothering me about this and I'm not sure what it is', 'That doesn't feel right', 'I know I should but . . .', or 'I know I shouldn't but . . .'

- Write down the pros and then the cons – both sides of the argument. Be honest – and get it all down. This is not a numbers game. One con could outweigh all the pros – or vice versa.

- Just by writing it all down, you'll bring everything to your conscious mind. Now you've done that, you should now know the answer to your own question.

Making sense now?

Your unconscious mind has already begun working out what this all means and how you can apply it to your own life. In your home life, your work life, your relationship, your social life. Once you get your conscious and unconscious singing the same tune, you'll make better decisions, you'll be happier, better stuff will seem to happen to you and you'll find yourself getting what you want.

There can be times when your conscious and your unconscious are at war and you don't even realize it. Meet Sandra. You might know someone like her. Sandra avoided looking in the mirror. She didn't want to see how fat she was. To put it a better way, she wanted to be thinner. Not lose weight. Be thinner. Sandra really wanted to be thinner, she thought. She wanted a figure more like the women she saw in *Vogue* magazine. Sandra's boyfriend, Gary, liked Sandra as she was. He loved her curvy shape. The first time he saw her, Gary fancied Sandra. And Sandra knew that. Gary told her he really fancied her. And she knew he meant what he said.

So why is Sandra still fat? How come she hasn't managed to get any thinner – apart from perhaps two pounds? She would like to be thinner. But do you think she wants to be thinner? Really? Does she need to be thinner?

Sandra would probably say that she wanted to be thinner. But deep down, a part of her – guess which part – knew there was a *benefit* to staying the way she was: the fact that Gary loved her that way. Her conscious mind and her unconscious mind were not saying the same thing and her unconscious was blocking her from getting the thing she thought she wanted – to be thinner.

Once you've learned to communicate better with your unconscious, one thing you'll be able to do is throw out any nasty habits. Like when I stopped smoking. I'd been talking about giving up cigarettes, but never got around to it. My conscious mind told me it was bad for me, expensive and antisocial but my unconscious saw some benefits. Deep down, I like being different, you see. I didn't like being told I should stop, and the fact that smokers were becoming more and more frozen out by non-smokers thrilled me in some strange way. My unconscious was telling me that smoking was in some way exciting and different – and a way of asserting my individuality.

In other words, I wasn't able to pack up smoking because my conscious and my unconscious were not in agreement. All I needed to do was go with one of them and convince the other one! I needed to decide – fully – either that I was happy to die young if it meant I could be different and rebellious, or that being different and rebellious was not worth risking an early grave for. I went with the second, telling myself that I could satisfy my unconscious by finding different ways of being an individual rather than smoking. As usual, my unconscious *was* right; I *do* need exciting ways to be different. It just chose the wrong one. That can happen sometimes.

---

## DO THIS

- Choose a habit you have that you should obviously and logically give up. For example, smoking, eating too much, drinking too much, shopping too much – you name it.

- Ask yourself 'What's the secret benefit of keeping this habit going?' There will be an answer to this. What do you get out of it?

- Ask yourself the same question again: 'How else does this habit benefit me?'

- Ask yourself 'What else could I do to get those benefits?'

- Decide when you're going to start doing those new things to get those old benefits – and keep that appointment.

The secondary benefit for Sandra was that Gary liked her chubby. Or, to put it another way, her unconscious was worried that Gary would not love her if she lost weight. So her unconscious made sure she kept eating. What she needed to do was focus on everything that Gary did love about her – not just her figure – and find new things for him to love too.

One final thing. If you kick out a bad habit, you must always replace it with a good one – otherwise you leave a void. Every void needs filling and if you leave it empty, you might find it gets automatically filled by another bad habit rather than a good one. So in my case I began going to the gym every day. Especially at the key time when I most wanted a cigarette – when I got home from work in the evening.

## Your unconscious – a demo

You must have heard people in the past saying things like 'trust your gut' or 'go with your instincts', if you're finding it hard to make a decision. You know what, they're right – except they don't know why they're right. You're going to find out how to make the most of your instincts so you can learn to trust them.

Your unconscious is like a sponge. To give you a flavour of how good your unconscious is at absorbing things, here's some of what you've picked up already:

- Being adaptable leads to success. Practise by changing your routines frequently.

- You need to adapt fast – and often – to be successful in today's world.

- Thinking is all about what you see, hear, feel and say to yourself in your mind.

- You can fix any fears yourself just by changing how you're thinking about them.

- Your unconscious is often right. That means whatever you know deep down, you should pay attention to.

Your unconscious also picks up on all kinds of tiny things in people. I'm not talking about body language. I'm talking about something far more sophisticated. It's about understanding what makes people tick.

The reason I'm not bringing in body language here is that most interpretations of body language are taken in isolation and often wrong. You're bound to have heard of that old chestnut: that crossing your arms means you're feeling defensive? Yet, how many times have you crossed your arms when you were not feeling defensive? Perhaps when it was just comfortable to do so? Or you were cold? And don't get me started on the idea that says if you twiddle with your hair when you're looking at someone it must mean you fancy them. I misread that one for years and I still wish it was true. But it isn't. Necessarily. Most ideas about body language are generalizations. What I'm talking about is something you already know. You've known it for years. But you've known it unconsciously, and you're about to know it consciously instead.

You know that feeling when you meet someone for the first time and you just know within an instant whether you like them or not? Ask yourself now – how do you know that? How do you decide? Answer – it's your unconscious at work. Let's see how powerful your unconscious is now.

---

**DO THIS**

How much information do you reckon your brain processes every second? Go on – have a guess. Try this. Remember this number – 7748. Repeat it to yourself three times. Now close your eyes and repeat that number out loud from memory. (Only if you're by yourself though. We don't want you to get locked up.)

Now remember this number – 7942747748 – and do the same again.

If you managed that, it was more difficult wasn't it?

Now try this – 67942747748.

Getting much harder, isn't it?

OK do this one – 6794 2747 748.

Yes, it's the same number as the one before, but easier to remember in groups of four digits or fewer, right?

Your conscious brain can process up to nine separate bits of info fairly comfortably at any one time. After that it has a bit of a meltdown.

Your five senses (seeing, hearing, feeling, smelling and tasting) are being bombarded with lots of information all the time. Take a moment now and ask yourself what you're seeing, hearing, feeling, smelling and tasting at this very moment. And then ask yourself the same question now that the moment has passed. What's new? I bet you're seeing, hearing, feeling, smelling or tasting something different already. In fact, I know you are because you're looking at a different part of this paragraph, which contains different words, right?

So, how many bits of information do you think the other part of your brain, your unconscious, processes at any given moment? Go on, have a guess.

Two million.

Per second.

I was at a party on Saturday night. The party was loud and

there were lots of people there. I was busy chatting away to my friends, and suddenly, from behind me, in another group of people, I heard my name mentioned. At that very moment, I heard not only what that person was saying about me, but *what he'd been saying before he mentioned my name.* I was not consciously aware of hearing what he'd been saying before he mentioned my name. I was busy chatting with my own friends! So how was it that I 'remembered' hearing what I thought I hadn't heard? Is this the mark of someone with superhuman hearing? No. Everyone can do this.

More or less everything you ever experience is filed in the unconscious part of your brain. That means the vast majority of things you have ever experienced in your whole life. And that's millions of bits of information. There is no such thing as not being able to remember something. All that happens when you think you can't remember something – no matter how hard you try – is that you haven't found the way to access that memory yet. In other words, you know it's filed somewhere but the conscious part of your brain doesn't know where to find it. A bit like knowing you've got something somewhere stashed away inside your house but you don't know where exactly.

Don't believe me?

## DO THIS

Think of a friend from your schooldays that you haven't seen or thought about since the day you left school. Go back as far as you can to as young as you can remember. Go on, think. Don't move on from this paragraph until you've got someone.

Now that you've got someone, what was it you remembered first? Their name, their face, their voice, their smell?

Whatever you answered just now, you can now see their face in your mind's eye, right? Now have a closer look at that face. Notice their hair. Glasses? Eyes? Expression? Take your time. You might see all this straight away or it might take two or three minutes. Don't worry about how long it takes you but make sure you get some really good pictures. It's worth it.

The next point is even more intricate. Try the next bit to see how far you can really go. If you don't think you can do it properly, skip it, turn the page and continue from there.

OK – what about the sound of the person's voice? While you're looking closely at the details of their face, replay the sound of their voice as if they're talking to you. What was it like in tone? Loud or soft? Accent? Friendly? Are they smiling now or frowning? Or has their expression changed in another way? How did this person make you feel?

And how easy is it to remember how you were feeling now that you're accessing this memory in detail? In fact, how is it making you feel now?

OK – now do this. Scan slowly down from the face to the rest of their body. Notice what they're wearing. Maybe it's a school uniform, maybe it's not. It doesn't matter. Keep scanning down until you get to their shoes. What colour are they? Style? Scuffed or shiny? Laces or slip-ons? Can you see socks? Can you see what those shoes are standing on? Probably you can. Because if you can see those shoes, you can see what's underneath the shoes. If you can see the floor or the ground then you can probably see other things too. Are you outside or inside?

Now here's the killer question: how long ago was it that you last thought about that person? And how long ago was it that you last thought about them in that sort of detail?

Where's this going? Where it's going is inside your unconscious so that you can continue to learn how to get what you want. When you get that instant feeling of dislike, or you just click instantly with someone, that's your unconscious mind remembering in a nanosecond everything you've ever experienced in your life and telling you what to expect of this person based on those experiences. In other words, it is noticing little facial expressions that you don't think you're picking up, little tics, micro-movements, hand gestures, flicks of the eyes, the changing colour of the cheeks, minute changes in perspiration levels, where their feet are pointing, the tone of their voice, their choice of words, the list goes on.

And here's how clever your brain is. It is running this information by all those other experiences you've ever had and is picking out trends. And woe betide that person if too much of this stuff is in any way similar to people who have turned out to be bad for you. Your brain tells you in an instant that you're probably not going to like them – or you probably *are* going to like them, if it's the other way round – by sending you that gut feeling.

**Remember This**

*Learn to trust your gut most of the time. That's how you get what you want from yourself.*

## Your autopilots

As you've just been reading, your unconscious is huge and can do many things. Whether you're awake or asleep, it's always on. Part of its job is to control your automatic behaviour – breathing, blinking, growth of hair and nails and the fact that you can probably balance on two feet without thinking about it, change gears in your car without looking, and ride a bike without stabilizers.

I should tell you a bit more about automatic behaviour – the things we call autopilots. Autopilots don't just fly planes when the pilot wants a rest, they also do a lot of stuff for you in your brain so you don't have to think about it.

There's so much going on in your brain that it has to be selective about what it focuses on and what it leaves you to do automatically. Good autopilots take on a lot of jobs to free up your mind so it can concentrate on more important things. Think about when you have a shower. Once you've turned on the water, what do you do next? Think about it, put yourself back in the shower now and notice the order you do things in. It's the same each time, isn't it?

What about when you walk into a department store or a big

shop? Which way do you turn after you walk through the door? You can bet it's the same way each time. It's usually to the left, by the way, but not for everyone.

And what about putting on your trousers? Which leg goes in first? And then there's the shoes. The list goes on.

Autopilots can be really useful. While you're busy putting on trousers, washing parts of your body, walking into shops or brushing your teeth, the conscious part of your brain is busy focusing on the really important stuff – like the day ahead or what you're actually going to buy in that shop. Autopilots are a great way for your brain to control habitual behaviour without thinking.

That's fine if the habitual behaviour is good. If it's bad, you can find yourself with some really mischievous autopilots like the ones that make you end up selling your car (remember Lisa? See pages 21–22). Or the ones that kick in when people intimidate you or make you nervous or unsure of yourself. Did I mention that I used to light up a cigarette whenever I picked up the phone, finished a meal or got home from work? I now hate smoking. Apart from when I've been drinking alcohol.

Bad autopilots can install themselves when you're not looking. Before you know it, they're in – like a computer virus – telling you to do things that aren't helpful at all. Your brain is designed to allow autopilots to install themselves easily because without the good ones life would be impossible. Trouble is, it's not so good at spotting the difference between a good one and a bad one.

Through the process of reading this book, you're learning how to identify and get rid of bad autopilots, and how to replace them with something better. Once you get it right, the effect of this on your life is nothing short of biblical. You get rid of autopilots by short-circuiting them.

One woman's problem was, she said: 'When my engine runs down, my drug of choice is food.'

Over time she realized what she was really hungry for: 'I'm hungry for balance . . . I'm hungry to do something other than work.'

That thought process took years, and her 'eureka' moment came as a result of the help of other people. Once she talked about it and got their views, things began to change. There was the short-circuit.

Here's what was really happening in her mind. The more she worked, the more she needed to balance her work with something else. In her case, that something else happened to be food. It could easily have been something else – like alcohol, tobacco or drugs – or tennis, working out at the gym or shopping. But she balanced her work with food.

Whenever she felt like work was getting on top of her, she reached for crisps. Too many. Those crisps weren't filling a hole in her stomach. They were filling a hole in her life! When you think about it, that's some autopilot. Take a step back and look at what was going on. The harder she worked, the more 'out of balance' she got. The more 'out of balance' she got, the more she ate. The more she ate, the fatter she became. At her peak, she weighed 237 pounds. That's nearly 17 stone. Or 108 kilos.

Actually it was obvious to me what was going on in her mind, just by listening to her words. She called food her 'drug', telling me that she knew, at some unconscious level, that she was addicted and had a destructive relationship with food. And – think about it – can you really be 'hungry' for balance? No. You can be desperate for balance, you can feel like you really need balance. You can be hungry for crisps, or a Big Mac or spaghetti. But you can't eat balance! With those four words 'I'm hungry for balance', she exposed that autopilot, that association, for all to see. Well, not all. Just me. And now you.

Her brain had made an unconscious connection with food as a substitute antidote to her work. She knew that each time she reached for a new bag of crisps, she would pile on more pounds. She knew she was damaging her health. She knew her self-esteem was being hit too. But *it made no difference.*

Autopilots don't care about logic or reason. They do what is good for you at a really deep level. They're almost always right about what they want to achieve for you, but sometimes they choose the wrong way to get it. In this case, the autopilot was giving this woman a work/life balance, which she definitely needed. But by choosing food as the way of getting that balance, in reality she became bigger and bigger.

What do most people do when they start getting fat? They go on a diet. That's if they know nothing about autopilots, of course. Have you ever thought about why there are so many different types of diet out there? New ones come out all the time, don't they? You'd think that if being thin was just about diet or exercise, more of us would look like Brangelina, wouldn't we? Well, from the neck down at least.

So this woman started dieting. It was a tough one and the pounds dropped off. She was a lean, mean, slimming machine and she looked great. When she thought she was thin enough, she stopped the diet and – you guessed it – out came those bags of crisps again. And back came those pounds.

It was only when she discovered – with help from others – what was really happening in her *mind* that she began to win not just each battle with her weight, but the whole war. Look again at what she said, once she understood what was going on.

'I'm hungry for balance ... I'm hungry to do something other than work.'

From that moment, the autopilot was on Death Row. She saw the association with food and that meant she could now kick this autopilot's backside. It was as though a choir of angels had started a chorus of 'Hallelujah' in her head (briefly replacing her internal voice, of course).

The result was that she changed her attitude to losing weight. She stopped using food as a balance against her work once she realized she wasn't actually getting balance from it. And she found other – better – things to do to give her life more balance.

She became much happier and her weight became stable.

This woman is Oprah Winfrey.

## Conclusion

An autopilot is a piece of repeated unconscious behaviour. To put it another way, a thing you do automatically – and repeatedly – without much or any thought.

Good autopilots are a shortcut to making your life easier, like your morning routine, driving a car, or playing a particular sport or musical instrument. They can also give you automatic confidence, courage and adaptability so that finding solutions to problems becomes second nature (this is starting to happen as you go through the process of reading this book – just keep reading). Bad autopilots cause misery, like the ones which make you eat or drink too much, smoke, stay with the wrong person, lose your patience easily or let people walk all over you. You're learning how to get rid of those too.

To get what you want, you need to get rid of bad autopilots and replace them with good ones. You identify bad autopilots by using external influences. That could be talking to other people, having new experiences, sleeping on a problem or reading this book. You replace them with good ones by doing something else – anything else. Keep repeating that until it becomes a new behaviour, and a new autopilot.

# 4

# Rulebooks

One of the things you're really going to need to be adaptable with is your rulebook. When I say your rulebook, I mean your set of principles and values. In other words, what you think is right and wrong. Everyone has a rulebook. Some of the principles and values in your rulebook are set in stone and you wouldn't want to change them. Maybe your family always comes first; you believe it's wrong to steal; you think it's good to help other people if they're in need. Other parts of your rulebook will run less deep – and you can be more flexible.

The problem is that your rulebook is almost definitely not the same as anyone else's. People's rulebooks differ according to their social background, culture, upbringing, education and experiences. Today's world of fast communication, social mobility, easy travel and mass migration means there are lots of people living among each other with different rulebooks. And if you expect to get what you want by assuming people behave according to your personal rulebook, then I've got news for you. You're mad. Stark raving.

Have a look at some examples of how different rulebooks can be. Ready? Deep breath. Some of these have been around for longer than others. How many of these have you come across? Which ones are you?

Is £50 a lot of money? Is £500 a lot of money? Is it polite to make eye contact with someone when you're talking to them? Is it rude to make eye contact with someone when you're talking to them? If someone buys you a drink, should you be grateful and thank them? If someone buys you a drink, should you consider that as their 'round' and be obliged to buy them one back before going home? Is it polite to arrive late? Is it rude to arrive on time? Is working full-time to pay for your child really putting your child first? Is it right to make your child go without by not going to work?

Is your working day finished at home time? Is your working day finished when you've finished your work? Is working late a form of dedication or bad time management? Is seeing a psychiatrist getting fixed or breaking down? Is a team player a great colleague or shy of accountability? Is promotion recognition or doing the job of two people? Are inquisitive neighbours nosy and intrusive or taking an interest in their community? Is holding the door open for a woman polite or patronizing?

Off sick with a cold – lazy shirker or considerate to others? Working from home – forward-thinking business sense or a licence to be lazy? Talking about your achievements – showing off or proof that you're good? Saying how much you earn – measure of success or a social faux pas? The success of others – to be celebrated or envied? The downfall of others – celebrate or mourn? Divorce – solution or failure?

Sacking your friends – professional or traitor? Not replying to emails – busy or rude? Lending money – is it OK to ask for it back or is the onus on the borrower to give it back? Charity – solving the problem or making it worse? Facebook – more contacts or less contact? Haggling – fun or not done? Keeping your word – old-fashioned or honourable? Heart on your sleeve – passionate or irrational? Men who cry – sensitive or weak? A drunken kiss with someone other than your partner – means nothing or means everything?

Dividing the bill – equal parts or 'I didn't have coffee'? 'I'm sorry, I don't like that' – honest or rude? Faking qualifications – winner or loser? Semi-finalist – winner or loser? Toyota Prius driver – selfless saviour or sanctimonious sod? Flirting – harmless fun or heartless tease? Mates with your staff – great boss or weak leader? Pay rise – 'If you don't ask, you don't get' or 'I shouldn't have to ask, they should offer'? You make a date, you stick to it – or flexibility is key? Brown-nosing – selling out or selling in? Jeans at work – creative or confusing?

Back-to-back meetings – doing lots or doing nothing? Having affairs – marriage saviour or marriage wrecker? Prison inmate – potential employee or no second chance? Favouritism – natural or unfair? Talkative children – precocious or bright? Staying in the closet – compromise or cop-out? Designer clothing – classy or common? Cities – to move into some day or to move out of some day?

Changing with the times – keeping up with others or losing sight of yourself? Sex with your friends – sleeping around or staying in touch? Tomato – fruit or vegetable? Paris Hilton – famous place or infamous person?

When rulebooks clash, it can be disastrous. People try to get what they want and end up getting exactly the opposite. To show you what I mean, here are two examples.

Tracy came from a part of town famous for its street market. In this area most people are known for their straight-talking approach. They're traditionally hard-working, no-nonsense types. Tracy was just like that. She enjoyed a few drinks and a laugh. At home, family was everything. She worked hard and ended up with a good job at a big company on the other side of town. She was popular at work and prepared to do anything in order to get on. Every day she made an effort to make small talk with someone senior. Some people would call that arse-kissing. Others would say it's a good career success strategy. You decide. Eventually she was promoted to a senior position, which gave her the power to hire and fire. She found that her straight-talking style fitted her new role, particularly when it came to firing.

No arguments, no skirting the issue: 'Here's your cheque. There's the door.'

That's a short version of saying: 'Your severance payment will be transferred to your bank account by the end of the month. Please collect your belongings from your desk and give your security pass to the Facilities Department on your way out. Please be aware that you are no longer employed by this company with immediate effect and as such will not be allowed access to this building or any other owned by this company. Thank you for your hard work and loyal service. May I take this opportunity to wish you every success for the future. See you down the pub later.'

If you're anything like me, you're probably wondering what

that last comment was all about. It was about exactly what I've just said – 'like me'. Tracy wanted to be liked.

As I've indicated, Tracy enjoyed a few glasses of Pinot Grigio with her mates. She had a lot of mates at work. In fact, most of her life – and her social life – revolved around her job. But, once she got her new senior position, that all began to change.

A friend of mine – and Tracy's – was shown the door by Tracy one afternoon. Roxy was really upset. She cried. Luckily Roxy wasn't the only one being shown the door, so she took comfort from the other casualties of the afternoon and the whole group of former employees went to the pub to drown their sorrows. I think they'd really rather have drowned Tracy.

When Roxy and her friends arrived at the pub up the road, Tracy was still in her office, working. As I said, she was a hard worker. It was in her blood. She was such a hard worker and loyal member of staff that if she'd been a stick of rock, she'd have had the company logo printed all the way through her. At the end of her typically long day, Tracy packed up her things, locked the filing cabinets and office door and trotted up to the pub for a few drinks.

As Tracy arrived at the bar, she found Roxy and the others propping it up, six drinks to the wind. Tracy went up to Roxy, put her arm round her and asked, in a sincere and sympathetic way, 'Are you all right?' Tracy meant what she said. The two of them had propped up the same bar together for years.

'Take your hand off me. I don't want to talk to you. You've just fired me,' Roxy replied.

Tracy saw no reason why she couldn't be friends with people she fired. That's what she wanted. It didn't occur to her that this was probably about the last thing Roxy wanted. This was a serious rulebook clash. So Tracy did not get what she wanted.

Let me tell you my second story. Have you ever been nibbled? You probably have but you didn't know it at the time. Nibbling is when someone tries to trick you by going back on an agreement.

I used to do a fair bit of business consultancy, which I liked. But I didn't know about nibbling. One client of mine, Roger, asked me to do a large piece of work for him overseas. He gave me the brief and I put together a detailed proposal.

He read the proposal and liked it. I negotiated the fee and agreed it on the phone. We confirmed that agreement by email.

His PA called me the following week and asked me to come in for a meeting to talk about the logistics of the project; it was in another country and I needed to do some research before I started it. Roger was not like Tracy in any way. He was not straight talking, he was not from the same part of town, he did not like a drink and he did not like to fire people face to face. Roger liked to get other people to do that for him. We talked for an hour or so about how we would proceed, who I needed to talk to within his company first, and what he wanted to get out of it. It wasn't until almost the end of the meeting that Roger suddenly asked for a huge reduction in the price. I'm not talking about a small discount. The reduction he wanted was so massive that I thought about having him sectioned.

Roger wanted a lot. Roger didn't get what he wanted.

I didn't know about nibbling at the time. Or much about rulebooks for that matter. I wanted the business to be conducted according to my rulebook, under the section marked 'Business'.

One of the rules in my book says that if you agree a price, you stick to it. If not, you'd better have a damn good reason. And nowhere in my rulebook does it say that it's fair to spring a last-minute haggle on someone who thinks they've come in to discuss a project that's already started. That's what my rulebook says. Yours may not. Roger's certainly doesn't. And that's OK now I know that different people have different rulebooks.

Here are the rulebooks of the people we've just been talking about.

### Tracy

Sacking your friends – professional
Working late – dedication
Promotion – recognition
The downfall of others – mourn
'I'm sorry I don't like that' – rude
Mates with your staff – great boss
Brown-nosing – selling in

### Roxy

Sacking your friends – traitor
'I'm sorry I don't like that' – honest

### Roger

Haggling – fun
Keeping your word – old-fashioned

**Me**

Haggling – not done (at that point)
Keeping your word – honourable

Which bits of Roxy's, Roger's, Tracy's and my rulebooks match yours?

---

**DO THIS**

1. Think of a time when you've been hard done by – or someone has not behaved how you expected them to.

2. Now you know what you know about rulebooks, what are the differences between your rulebook and this person's?

3. Now that you know that – and about adaptability, too (see chapters 1 and 2) – what would you do differently if you had that time again?

4. Only answer question 3 if it still matters. You might find that it doesn't any more.

---

Mike, an English banking executive I know, went for a meal in a revolving restaurant at the top of a skyscraper in New York. It was a fancy restaurant with good food and good service. In England the standard tip in a restaurant is between 7 and 10 per cent. If we really enjoy ourselves, or if we want to impress our first date (only the first date), we'll make it a bit more. Apart from in restaurants where service is included, of course. In America, service is never included and people often tip as much as 20 per cent and the service is much better than in England. Mike enjoyed his meal as he spun around at the top of the skyscraper and doubled what he would normally give as a tip, putting down a whopping 15 per cent on top of the bill. The waiter asked: 'Was there anything wrong with your meal, sir?' How rude. Mike or the waiter, though?

Technology has changed, and continues to change, the way we communicate with each other. Ten years ago, you probably wouldn't have understood this:

> **Remember This**
> *One of the things that can prevent you getting what you want is the fact we all have different rulebooks. Some of what you do to persuade people will work. At other times, you'll be disappointed. When that happens, it probably means the rulebooks are clashing. To stop this getting in the way of what you want, you just need to know that rulebooks exist. That means you're ready for the unpredictable and you're prepared to be adaptable. Even if that sometimes means breaking your own rulebook.*

aunt g – thx 4 xmas prez. how r u? out l8 w/ m8s. Drnk agn – lol:) cu 2mrw xx

Technology has also affected people's rulebooks and the way they behave. It's easier to behave badly by email or text. And much harder to persuade people. You need to be face to face. People are more likely to stick to their own rulebooks when they're face to face with you – and that's important when it comes to influencing them or persuading them.

Being face to face makes it harder for people to say no to you, or shaft you, because they know they will *see* the consequences, your reaction, your disappointment. Now that people can avoid face-to-face interaction much of the time, it's easier for them to behave in a way that you – and your rulebook – would not usually expect from another human being. So, where possible, limit their options and meet face to face. People behave better face to face, and are more likely to give you what you want.

Did you see *Braveheart*? Do you remember those scenes of English and Scottish soldiers grabbing hold of each other, looking each other in the eye and trying to kill each other? OK, Mel and his mates were using a bit of Hollywood licence. Close combat like that had long since fallen out of favour when the real Robert the Bruce was marauding his way around Hadrian's Wall. Most people had graduated to longbows and crossbows by then. Now, in the modern world, close-quarters combat hardly exists at all. Why? Because it makes life easier, and it makes death easier – that's why. Imagine for some reason you are forced to kill someone. I hope you wouldn't want to – but imagine for some reason you are forced to and there's no getting out of it. I mean I want you to imagine – hypothetically – that you have to bring about someone's untimely demise. How would you rather do it?

**DO THIS**

Please choose one from the list below – hypothetically!

- Choke them to death with your bare hands; be deafened by their screams, watch their eyes bulge from their sockets and feel their last breath on your face.

- Shoot them from long range with a sniper rifle. See – through the rifle's scope – their tiny figure fall dead on the ground.

- Launch a missile from the comfort of your own home by pressing a red button. Receive a written report that your missile attack has been successful, your target is dead and that there have been no other civilian casualties.

- Pay someone else to kill them. Let them decide how, when and where it happens – you only want to hear back from them once it's all over.

I said hypothetically – so you have to pick one of them. Which is it to be? I think I know. Remember, you are more predictable than you think.

Your principles and values – in your rulebook – run deep. That's why they are principles and values – rather than just beliefs, which tend not to run so deep and are more easily changed. Breaking your own principles or values feels like you're betraying yourself as a person. The reason I chose the example above is because (I hope) that you and nearly everybody else has a core principle that it is wrong to kill another human. I know there may be exceptions – especially in a military context. But in the main, most people could not – and would not – break this core principle. But they could. Here's how.

If you absolutely have to, it's far easier to go against one of your core principles – even one as strong as not wanting to kill someone – if you are desensitized from what's going on. Compare the first example of choking someone to death. What would your five senses make of it? Now go to the end example of paying someone to do it for you. What would you see, hear, feel, smell or taste of that person dying? Nothing. Even if you chose the missile option, you'd get a huge reduction in the way you responded emotionally, but you would still feel your finger on the red button and you would know that the sensation of pushing that button was going to lead to someone's death.

> **Remember This**
>
> *Everyone has different rulebooks, but that's only half the story. Electronic, faceless communication means they're finding it easier and easier to break their own rulebooks without feeling guilty. So never make assumptions based on your own rulebook about other people or how they might behave.*

So – what's all this got to do with getting what you want? Let me go back to technology. To email, Facebook, Twitter, MSN, texting, YouTube, chat forums, Second Life, LinkedIn, Spoke, MySpace, eBay, and vlogging. If you can't – or you can barely – see, hear, feel – and to a lesser extent, smell or taste – the person you're talking to, then how much easier is it to break your own rulebook? How much easier still if you don't know their real name or even whether they're a man or a woman? That means not only can you not see them for real, you can't see them in your mind's eye either!

And if people are communicating with each other like this – as they are a lot – then guess what, they're not sticking to their own rulebooks either. Ridiculous when you think about it – they don't even know they've got these rulebooks and they're breaking them already.

I have a graphic memory of being dumped by a girlfriend when I was younger – in my acne phase. She watched me squirm, she listened to me beg for forgiveness, she felt me pull desperately at her sleeve one last time, she smelt my Polo – by Ralph Lauren – and she tasted the double Southern Comfort and lemonade I'd bought her by way of bribery.

Now I look back, it can't have been too easy for her either. Nobody likes to see a half-grown man cry. Whatever. I know she would have found it easier to dump me by text. If it had existed at the time.

I'd never have got a chance to talk her round if she'd dumped me by text. As it turned out, all my efforts paid off and we ordered another couple of Southern Comforts and lemonade. The next thing we knew, two more weeks had passed and we were still together.

So next time someone behaves badly or in a way you don't consider acceptable, or if they surprise you by behaving in a way you don't expect, it's either because they have a different rulebook or they are at enough distance from you to be able to break their own rules. Usually by email or text.

## Conclusion

Everyone has a rulebook – a set of values, principles and beliefs. Everyone's is different, based on their culture, background and experiences. People who do not think about this find it much harder to get what they want. You need to know this so you can be ready to adapt when people surprise you and behave in an unexpected way.

To get what you want, stay adaptable. Being adaptable means you will succeed. Expect the unexpected because your rulebook is not the same as other people's. Face-to-face communication is the best way of getting what you want.

# 5

# What Matters and What Doesn't

We've talked a lot about being adaptable and how it leads to success. But that doesn't mean adapting to the wrong things. You need to adapt to what matters and ignore what doesn't matter. Even better is to learn how to get rid of things that don't matter, so you can concentrate on what does. Here are some examples from both of us.

I can remember when winning the hundred metres at school was my life. If I didn't win the hundred metres, then I might as well have stopped living.

*And I can remember risking detention after detention trying to get out of the hundred metres. Anything to get away early and watch television.*

I came second every time. And always to Simon Rowley. But I had this theory that he only won because his face was more aerodynamic than mine. You know the type.

Every school has one. When he had his ears pinned back by the doctor, I even swore at the time it was so he could win the hundred metres. That's how obsessed I was. Now that I'm older, I know different. I now realize I was slowed down by the half-inch-thick layer of acne cream I had to slap all over my forehead every day. Oh I'm digressing (as well as regressing). Well it did say 'apply liberally'.

*I got caught walking home from school in the middle of the day when I was supposed be at PE. Funny, I go to the gym a fair bit these days. I can't think why I was so desperate to avoid exercise back then. It's good to look back and realize now that none of this matters any more. And now that it's passed, I'm past caring. I've got the presence of mind to know that, sooner or later, however tense the present is making you, you are probably already aware of how much things have changed since the past and how quickly the future becomes the past.*

You know that last sentence was mildly confusing. It was one of those times when you were supposed to be a bit confused. I distracted you so that you could learn a key point easily at a subconscious level: however big a problem seems, there will usually come a time when it doesn't matter any more. So whenever something's bothering you, just imagine the time in the future when it won't matter any more – or when it will matter a lot less than now – and you'll feel better about it straight away. Solving problems like this is an example of being very adaptable, as you're about to find out.

## DO THIS

- Think of something that used to get to you or bother you in some way. It doesn't matter how long ago – but the more recent it was, the better.

- Ask yourself, now that you look back at it, how come it no longer matters? What's changed?

- What do you know now that – if you'd known about it at the time – would have made sure this thing would never have mattered in the first place?

## NOW DO THIS

- Now do it for something that gets to you or bothers you now. Imagine you've moved forward to a time when it no longer matters (maybe that's six months/a year/two years – but no longer).

- Now that you're in this future position and looking back at it, ask yourself how come it no longer matters? What's changed?

- What advice can you give yourself from this future position to help it not matter to you back there in the present?

Getting what you want can often be blocked by things you allow to prey on your mind. Things that appear to be important or urgent at the moment. If you're feeling down or distracted, you'll find it harder to focus on what you want. Getting rid of what's bothering you by doing the previous exercise will clear some space in your mind so you can think about your priorities.

Now that you can look back and look forward whenever you want to, let's leap back to the Millennium Bug. Remember that? I've almost forgotten myself. What was it again? Well, it wasn't – that's the point. But apparently it was going to be planes dropping out of the sky, nuclear missiles going off left, right and centre, free cash from the ATM and rogue dish-washers roaming the streets.

Experts around the world told us that machines would go haywire and that the world could end as soon as the clock struck midnight on 31 December 1999 because computers wouldn't be able to cope with the following year starting with a 2.

But nothing happened.

# 6

# Plan

If you're anything like me, there are bound to have been times in your life when you've thought about something you'd like, but you said to yourself 'What's the point? I've got no chance.' Or perhaps you thought it *was* possible, but never got round to doing anything about it. You've probably had times when you've had a rough idea of something you want – but nothing concrete.

Plus – and this was my default way of thinking for a very long time – it's really easy to *think* you're thinking about something you want, when in fact you're thinking about something you don't want. And those two are not the same thing.

A key part of getting what you want is to set a clear and

defined objective first, before you take any action. This chapter is designed to help you think about what you do want and how to create a process to flesh out the detail of that objective to give you the best possible chance of achieving it.

Let's take each thought process that I've just mentioned, one at a time, and look at it in more detail.

When you say to yourself 'What's the point? I've got no chance', it means your internal dialogue and pictures are joining forces to make you think of yourself failing. That means seeing yourself fail, telling yourself you're failing, and feeling like a failure.

When you find yourself not really sure about what it is you want, or you find yourself not getting round to taking any action to achieve it, your brain's thinking about things in a different way. It usually means your internal dialogue isn't saying very much and your internal pictures are vague, unclear and not very vivid.

And when you're thinking about what you *don't* want – well, that gets your brain thinking about the wrong thing entirely. And, worse, that means your unconscious starts to focus on all the wrong ideas.

Most people know what they don't want. If you ask what they *do* want, they will often talk about what they don't want. Ask someone what they would change about their appearance, if they could and they'll tell you what they don't like about themselves. They'll tell you they don't like their legs, their tummy, their nose or their figure. And if you ask someone what they like on the menu, they'll often answer by telling you what they don't like.

Here's what can happen if you focus too much on what you don't want. My nephew's best friend, Noah, has got a small scar on the palm of his left hand. His mum, Sasha, hates ironing. She would prefer to have someone else do it but Sasha's husband, Warren, says it's a waste of money. The phone rang while Sasha was doing her ironing. No, she does know the difference between the phone and the iron . . . it's not that story.

She told Noah not to go near the iron. Now you know how Noah got his scar. Noah hadn't even noticed the iron. He was playing with his Lego.

Telling Noah not to touch the iron made him think about touching the iron. It hadn't occurred to him before that. For the human brain *not* to think about something, it has to think about it first. Don't think about what colour underwear the Prime Minister is going to wear tomorrow. Impossible, isn't it?

That means if you say to yourself 'I don't want this', and 'I don't want that', you'll get your brain thinking about the thing you don't want. And that's the wrong thing to be thinking about. That's why people who focus on *not* being in debt, *stopping* smoking, *not* being fat and *avoiding* Mr Wrong very often end up with exactly what they don't want. If that's you, start thinking about it in this way now: being *in* credit, choosing to *be* healthy, *becoming* slimmer and *finding* Mr Right. Your brain will start making the *right* pictures and words then – and your unconscious will start doing the rest.

Do you like heights? I don't. If you don't, don't look down. I said don't! I don't mind heights now because I make sure I look up. Or even straight ahead.

Back to what you want (rather than what you don't want).

I can confirm you're now ready to start talking positively about what it is you want. I'm giving you the nod to move on and go straight to getting what you want. It's all adding up now. What do you really want?

---

**DO THIS**

- Think about something that's bothering you. Something that might begin with 'I don't want . . .' Or 'I wish I didn't . . .' Or 'I wish there wasn't . . .'

- Now flip it over. Flip it into the thing you *do* want instead. It's normally the opposite of the thing you don't want. This makes it something you want to go *towards* rather than move *away from*.

- Now do it again with something else.

- Notice the difference in how you feel when you start saying things in terms of what you *do* want rather than what you *don't* want.

---

Now you know how to think about what you do want, you simply need to practise until it becomes a habit. If you catch yourself saying 'I don't want . . .' then just stop and rephrase. But, what happens if the thing you say you want seems impossible or unattainable? And if that impossible, unattainable thing seems like the only option and you find yourself saying 'What's the point?'

Let me tell you about my niece, Megan. She's a really talented singer. And she writes her own songs. She should make a career out of it. I'm sure she's good enough.

Megan would love to win *X Factor*. It's her dream. Everything she's done up to this moment has been about getting on the programme. She's been singing since she was three and music is in her blood. My gran says she has the voice of an angel. She wants to win *X Factor* for her mum. It's been such a journey – an emotional roller coaster – but if she wins *X Factor*, she'll be living her dream. She's going to tidy her bedroom specially so that when the cameras come round they can get a good view of the toy microphone she used to sing into when she was five. She's come so far. If she doesn't win *X Factor*, she'll be devastated. I hope she wins, because it sounds like it's game over if she doesn't. Why does she want to win so badly? Because she wants limos to drive her around. She wants to be able to cry in front of millions of people. She wants crowds gathering in the main square of her home town and she wants her old primary schoolteacher to say what a great pupil she was.

She wants the life of a megastar and all the trappings that brings. She wants a hit single. What's wrong with *Britain's Got Talent*? Or if you really want to go for it – *American Idol*? Or *America's Got Talent*? Or there's that bloke I know. Well he's my brother's mate, really. He runs a hotel in Spain. He might be able to help, if she can talk him round. He hires entertainment every season. Or she could get herself an agent, couldn't she? Or she could launch herself on MySpace. Or YouTube. Or she could sing in the shower really loudly every morning with the window open and hope a passing A&R man discovers her. Or she could just carry on practising at the Duke of York pub on Thursday nights. They do a nice line in retro sandwiches, I hear.

Let me put it another way. Winning *X Factor* is not really what she wants. What she *really* wants is to be a famous singer, and ideally end up with a celebrity lifestyle. *X Factor* is one way of getting that – but if she could get it another way, that would be just as good. If *X Factor* is one way of fulfilling her dream, she needs at least two more if she's serious. Because she will only ever have a real choice – and a real chance – if she gives herself three options. If she sticks with just the one option, she's putting all the control in the hands of one other person (in this case, Simon Cowell, and who wants to do that?). High stakes mean high desperation. And you never get what you want if you're desperate.

There's a whole raft of reasons why you don't get what you want if you're desperate and fixed on only one way of getting it. If you're desperate, you'll come across as desperate. That's your unconscious being a big-mouth and sending off all those non-verbal signals you can't control. If you find yourself feeling desperate, or saying 'I can't help it, I *am* desperate', adjust your internal pictures and your internal dialogue. Make sure you create some good pictures of the options you *could* have to get what you want. And make sure your internal dialogue is talking about those various options – and how any of them would be good enough to get you what you want.

Having three choices means you won't be desperate. It means you're ready to walk away from option number one and try number two or three instead. That'll change the way you come across and how people perceive you unconsciously. If you've got this far and you've still only got one option as a way of getting what you want, then you need more.

If you give yourself an extra option, you still only have two. That's a dilemma. Sometimes that's even worse. It means you're in doubt. You're unsure. You end up stuck. And you don't do anything. You don't get what you want.

That's why you need three options. My niece's three need to be the ones most likely to work. The most important ones. I've had a chat with her and now she will apply for *X Factor*. She's also going to put her songs on MySpace. And meet my brother's mate who runs the hotel in Spain.

---

### DO THIS

Give yourself a proper choice every time. Do this whenever you want something.

- Think of something you really want.

- Think of the most obvious way of getting that.

- Now think of two more ways of getting it.

---

Even if it seems like you only have one option, you can always generate another and then another. Think of what else would 'tick the boxes' that your first option ticks. Don't move on to going after what you want until you have three possible ways of going after it.

---

**DO THIS**

This is how you decide what you want and how you're going to get it. Ask yourself:

1. What is going on at the moment that I don't like?

2. What do I want instead?

3. When am I going to do something about that? And what? (There are always answers to these; do not move on until you've answered them.)

4. Who's the most important person I need to persuade first to help make this happen?

5. If I can't persuade that person, who else can I persuade to make this happen?

6. How am I going to know when I've got what I want?

---

For example, here's how my niece would answer those questions in her quest for global domination of the pop charts.

1. What is going on at the moment that I don't like? (I've got a great singing voice and I'm really talented but I can't seem to get a break as a singer.)

2. What do I want instead? (I want to be a professional singer. Hopefully that will lead eventually to the lifestyle of a megastar and all the trappings that brings.)

3. When am I going to do something about that? And what? (I'm going to phone my uncle on Tuesday the 29th and get the number of his friend who runs a hotel in Spain.)

4. Who's the most important person I need to persuade first to help make this happen? (My uncle's friend with the hotel in Spain.)

5. If I can't persuade that person, who else can I persuade to make this happen? (Other people who run hotels that provide entertainment.)

6. How am I going to know when I've got what I want? (I will be singing professionally – in other words, I'll be paid for singing – and people will start to refer to me as a professional singer.)

The man with the hotel in Spain is called Grant Robinson.

# 7

# Get Inside Their Head

You've decided what you really want and you've decided on who's the most important person to influence first. In Megan's case, in the previous chapter, it was to be a singer and the most important person to influence first was the man with the hotel in Spain, Grant Robinson.

Now, before you do anything else, you need to strike first. Here's why. If you let others strike first, they might get what they want instead and you might not get what you want at all. You might even get the opposite of what you want. This means making the first move and preparing for the conversation in a particular way. It means taking the lead, thinking first, and then acting first. If you start second, you'll probably come second, or third. It would be an uphill struggle from that moment to get what you want. You'd be on the back foot. You could still get what you want from that position but you'd have to be on top form to do that. Or you'd have to have read this book at least twice.

Megan's going to meet Grant. To prepare for the meeting,

she needs to get inside his head, even though she's never met Grant before in her life. To do that, she needs to ask herself some specific questions. OK, Megan, step into Grant's head now.

*(Airport-style announcement) Welcome to Grant's head. While you're in here, please steer clear of those dark memories from his childhood. Please answer the following questions – and remember not to be restricted by your own rulebook:*

Megan, over to you. Just answer the questions as if you were Grant.

Who are you? (*Grant Robinson, hotel manager in Benidorm.*)

What do you do? (*I'm in charge of recruiting and managing entertainment staff. Some I advertise for – others approach me.*)

When you talk to Megan, what do *you* want? (*I want to discover talented new singers and other acts. But the majority of 'singers' who approach me are no good.*)

Why do you want that, Grant? (*It's my job. I want to look good in front of my boss. And I get a commission from entertainment sales so if I discover a great act, I get more money.*)

Why might you want to stop Megan getting what she wants? (*She might not be any good. She might not be different enough compared with the acts I've already got. We might not get on with each other. I might not have the budget to hire her.*)

If you decided to stop Megan getting what she wants, how would you do it? (*I could tell her to send me some recordings of her work – but then never get back to her. I could listen to her work and tell her I don't think it's a goer. I could agree to meet her but then cancel the meeting if something better came along in the meantime. I could meet her and fob her off with empty promises, and then never get back to her.*)

How and where will you be having the conversation? (*Initially by email or phone. If I decide to meet her, we'll hold an audition at the hotel*).

What's the best way for Megan to persuade you to give her what he wants? (*She needs to persuade me that she can sing, and also that she stands out from the crowd as a singer. She needs to show me what's different about her. She needs to show me that we can work together, and that she's reliable. And she needs to be willing to do it for quite a low fee.*)

Just by asking herself those questions, Megan now knows a lot more about Grant – how to persuade him and what to look out for if he tries to throw obstacles in her way and not play fair. Her answers may not be 100 per cent accurate but that's not a problem. The very fact that she's taken the time to think about what makes him tick, rather than just what *she* wants, means she's now got a much better plan in her mind than most people would have.

Before she even picks up the phone to Grant, here's what Megan is going to do that she wouldn't have thought about doing if she hadn't made the effort to get inside Grant's head. She knows that it's not enough simply to be a good singer. She needs to find out what other acts he has on his books already so she can work out how she can stand out from them. She knows she needs to spend time choosing the songs – and any photographs – that she's going to send him to make her sound and look different. She also needs to think about how little money she's prepared to work for – if it means getting her first break as a singer.

The key to getting inside someone's head is to imagine you *are* them.

Your turn.

---

### DO THIS

Decide on something you want and who is the most important person you need to influence first. Step inside the person's head. Imagine you *are* them and answer the same questions – coming up again now.

1. Who are you?

2. What do you do?

3. When you talk to —, what do YOU want?

4. Why do you want that?

5. Why might you want to stop — getting what s/he wants?

6. If you decided to stop — getting what s/he wants, how would you do it?

7. How and where will you be having the conversation?

8. What's the best way for — to persuade you to give her/him what s/he wants?

What did you learn about that person? What insight have you got into that person – and what they want – that you didn't have before?

## Conclusion

Decide what you *do* want instead of what you *don't* want. Come up with at least three ways of getting it. One or two are not enough. Decide who you need to influence first.

Get inside their head and figure out what they want before you talk to them. Work out how you can best use those insights to help you get what you want. Decide how you're going to know once you've got what you want.

# 8

# Got the T-shirt

You know about your internal pictures and how you can make sure you get the right ones and not the wrong ones (see pages 24–28). You know you can choose what you see – and how you see it – in your mind's eye. Now it's time to put that into practice and use your visualization skills to adjust your beliefs. From now on, picture everyone you want to influence wearing a particular T-shirt. If you're a bit of a fashionista, by all means make it Gucci or Prada or Primark. Whatever you want, as long as it's a good one. The T-shirt says:

> *I've been persuaded before*
> *I can be persuaded again,*
> *and again, and again . . .*

The T-shirt principle works because it presupposes that everyone is persuadable at any point in time. Or to persuade you that this is true: getting what you want means you just need to persuade people in the right way.

But first, you need to make the T-shirt. In your mind's eye, of course. Choose the colour. Choose the style – tight or baggy? What does the writing look like? What colour is the writing? How big is it? Can you make it bigger? What's it made from? What does it feel like? Got it? That's the T-shirt you're going to see everyone wearing when you need to influence them. Pick a person now – someone you want something from – and see them wearing that T-shirt.

Now stop thinking about the T-shirt. Think about a dog. Now think of your person in the T-shirt again.

Do that again. Think of a potato. Now think of the person in the T-shirt again.

One last time. Think of a telephone. Now think of the person in the T-shirt.

It's probably easy now to think about the T-shirt quickly and automatically. Remember – this really is a case of one size fits all. Everyone's going to be wearing it. Everyone you want to persuade, that is.

To reassure you that I've not lost my mind, here's why the T-shirt principle is so important. It's all about beliefs. Beliefs are a lot more than you believe them to be. Most of what you think you know is actually just a strongly held belief. In the same way as people used to think they knew it was impossible to get a written message from New York to Paris in a matter of seconds. Until it became possible – and now we all know you can. You've probably believed things strongly before that you no longer believe. Like I did: remember when I believed that winning the hundred metres was the most important thing in the world (see pages 61–62)? There are almost definitely things you thought you knew for a fact that you now no longer believe.

The point is – your strongly held beliefs are behind almost everything you do. Your rulebook (see chapter 4) is your set of beliefs. You can call the strong beliefs in your rulebook 'values' and 'principles' – and some of them will be so strong and apparently unchangeable that you think they can't possibly be just a belief. They make up who you are. And, more importantly, what you do. But ultimately, they're just beliefs. And if you really want to, you can change them. Or add new ones.

You form new beliefs all the time. Most of your major ones were formed when you were very small with the help of your parents, teachers, etc. You create new beliefs throughout your life, based on your experiences, without realizing. Think about something you believe this year that you didn't believe last year – based on something that's happened. And last month? Or yesterday? I believe that global warming is real now. Last year, I didn't.

Here's where you come in. Rather than just sitting back and letting beliefs form in your mind based on what happens to you, why not get up and decide what beliefs you want to have? The ones that are going to get you doing stuff that's good for you. To get you the things you want.

When I was young, I was at school with a boy, Paul, who was always in the shadow of his younger brother, Graham. Graham was by far the better footballer and was brilliant in the classroom. He thought at the time that football was the key to success. Their father was really proud of him – and there was no doubt who was his favourite. Paul knew his brother was the lucky one and that he himself was just ordinary. No one took much notice of him, at home or at school. He just blended into the background. Until computers came to the classroom.

Big, bulky ones they were. I'm not sure how much they could do back then but, whatever it was, Paul turned out to be a natural at making them do it. He spent hours in front of the screen, writing programs and making up games. He soon became known in school for it. He was probably one of the first people to get into gaming, even though he didn't know it at the time.

Nowadays, Paul wouldn't dream of blending into the background. If you met Paul and Graham, you'd never believe that one had once been far more confident and successful than the other. Paul even talks, walks and dresses differently now. Because he knows things about himself that he didn't know before. Which means he behaves differently. Things are much better for him. More people like him and he seems to have more luck. In other words, once he was able to choose a better thing to believe about himself, once he 'knew' he was good at something, his life became very different.

I want you to choose one belief. And I want you to know that everyone might as well be wearing a T-shirt that says

> *I've been persuaded before*
> *I can be persuaded again,*
> *and again, and again . . .*

Holding on to that belief will have an effect on how persuasive you come across. That's not just my belief. That's a fact.

A belief is a thing you choose to believe, either consciously or unconsciously. Once it's there, you behave according to it. You can choose to make or break a belief at any time. Choosing a good one will have you behaving in a way that gets you what you want. Choosing to believe that everyone has been persuaded before, and can be persuaded again and again, will change your unconscious behaviour and communication. In other words, just choosing this belief means you won't have to think too much about what you say and how you come across. It will happen automatically and dramatically increase the likelihood of you getting what you want.

Many of your words, pictures and behaviours are normally controlled by autopilots (see pages 41–46). If you consciously choose the right internal words and pictures, you'll have an immediate effect on how you feel and come across. Getting into the habit of doing this will create more good autopilots and replace any bad ones. Now you've got the T-shirt, you've adapted. You've got the right belief to get what you want.

PS: if you choose to believe that someone cannot be persuaded, then you'll be right.

# 9

# Persuasion Technique Number 1: Getting Connection

You know how it feels when you just 'click' with someone? Getting connection is 'clicking' with people on purpose. Persuading people you 'click' with is much easier than persuading anyone else.

Your brain is constantly, unconsciously, processing a staggering amount of information about people. A lot of that information is non-verbal – like facial expressions and the way people stand, sit, walk and move. So let's leave the talking out of it for now and focus on the non-verbal stuff. And that's a lot, believe me. I'm not going to sit here and bang on about the percentage of non-verbal communication in humans versus verbal communication. You probably know that most of the stuff that counts is non-verbal.

We're going to split people into three parts. Their face, their body and their legs. Check out these lists for an idea of all the different ways that people communicate without knowing they're doing it. Don't worry, this is just to give you a flavour, you don't have to learn them by heart.

## Face

Eyes – squinting, wide open, rapid blinking, staring into space, looking up/down to the right or down to the left, pupil dilation, darting in different directions. Head – tilted to the left/right, hanging down, nodding/shaking frequently or intermittently/quickly or slowly, pulled back, flushed/rash on neck. Face – cheek colour flushed/pale, eyebrows raised/pointing down/towards the middle, perspiration levels, nostrils flared, creased forehead, jutting/clenched jaw, wrinkled nose, breathing through mouth or nose, licking lips, smiling, frowning, pursed lips, swallow rate, biting lip, dry or moist lips, smiling with mouth but not eyes, grinding of teeth, lip colour.

## Body

Hands – gesticulating frequently/seldom, pointing, half pointing, clenched fist(s), hands clasped in front, cracking knuckles, fingers together/palms apart, hands hanging down by their side, touching face/other parts of body, fiddling with pen/object, biting nails, palm perspiration, hands in pockets, scratching/itching/ picking, twiddling thumbs, sitting on hands, palms down, hands on hips, hand on chin. Arms – outstretched, behind head, crossed, behind back, symmetrical/asymmetrical position, one arm resting on the other, down by one side, elbow(s) on table, goose pimples. Shoulders – hunched, back, shrugging (frequency), forward, turned to one side, still and without movement, one higher than the other. Chest – out, in, breathing rapidly, slowly, staccato, deep, shallow.

## Legs

Legs – crossed, apart, twitching, jiggling, splayed, both bent, both straight, one bent, one straight, stretching. Feet – wide apart, close together, crossed, both pointing in the same direction (right/left), pointing in opposite directions, pointing at what/who, wiggling toes, raised on floor, resting up on object, standing on balls/heels, rocking backwards and forwards/side to side, tapping one/both, direction in relation to rest of body, slow considered movements, walking on balls/heels.

What you must remember, though, is that taking any one of these non-verbal signs in isolation is wrong and can lead to all kinds of incorrect assumptions. Just like the old 'folding my arms means I'm defensive' rubbish that I mentioned earlier (see page 36).

The idea is to teach your conscious mind to be more aware than it's ever been of what's going on with another person. There are numerous combinations in the above examples of what people do with their bodies. Your unconscious mind knows what those combinations mean and can process them in an instant. So-called body language books go wrong because they tell you to take one of these things in isolation and form an assumption from it.

The really clever stuff happens when you start to notice some of these signs *consciously* too. Then your awareness of people goes through the roof.

## DO THIS

We're going to pick one item from each of the Face, Body and Legs sections for you to play with now. To look at the tilt of the head, whether the fingers are scratching or picking and what the feet are pointing at for the moment.

Look at another person – it doesn't matter if you know them or not – and pay attention to their head, hands and feet. You could do it in a shop or a bar or on a train. It's better if they're not aware of what you're doing. Is the head tilted? In which direction? What are the fingers doing? Where are the feet pointing?

Don't worry about anything else at the moment. Just focus on these. Don't worry about what you think it means. This is to start you off exercising the conscious part of your brain in an area usually dominated by the unconscious part. Obviously I don't need to tell you that your conscious brain is like a muscle. The more you exercise it, the more you develop it.

Once you've done that, pick another three signs – any three you like this time as long as it's one from each category – and do the same.

Now make a point of always noticing three pieces of non-verbal information about anyone and everyone you ever meet for the rest of your life. Notice how you start to pick up on so much more than just three bits of info. Once this becomes second nature, pick another three and look for those. The more you do this, the easier it gets. That's how you get your brain tuned to picking up non-verbal information consciously rather than just unconsciously.

So that's how you bring some of what your unconscious notices in people into your conscious. Your awareness of people will go through the roof. But it's the tip of the iceberg. Your unconscious soaks up much more.

---

**ALERT!** *How to achieve exactly the opposite of what this book is intended to achieve –*

Some people can be really annoying. One such person, let's call him Frank, learned a fraction of this material and thought it was enough. He spent his time staring at people to try to pick up on their non-verbals. They thought he was clinically insane. We all did. You can pick up on non-verbals from as far away as across the street. You never need to stare like Frank did. And, anyway, we'll be introducing you to your peripheral vision next.

---

To give an idea of how much non-verbal information your brain picks up unconsciously, let me tell you about what happened the other day. I was having lunch with a friend, Tony. He didn't realize how powerful his unconscious mind is.

'Go on, prove it to me,' he said.

So I said to Tony, 'OK, don't look round, but how many people do you reckon are sitting at the table behind you?'

I should say that he had not consciously looked at or taken any notice of the table behind him. I could see it, though, because I was sitting opposite him.

'No idea, five? Maybe a family?'

It was exactly five. Two adults and three kids. Of course Tony had seen it. He just didn't know he'd seen it.

Here's what it's all about. Your peripheral vision is highly developed and programmed to spot even the tiniest of movements from a long way off. If only you'd pay attention to the part of your brain that has ensured your survival for millions of years rather than the part – clever as it is – that's been knocking around for just a fraction of that time. Your unconscious is old and wise. Your eyes can see things everywhere – left, right and centre. And down. But not up. Man has never had anything to fear from the skies. He never had to look up for danger. Unless he happened to be under a very large tree that had been struck by lightning but that didn't happen very often.

---

**DO THIS**

Use your peripheral vision

Wherever you're sitting or standing or lying down reading this book, I want you to listen to only me now. And I want you to read only each word that you've got to on the page as it comes – one at a time – and no further. Stop now that you've got to the word 'further'. You can see into the future without even trying, can't you? You already know what I'm going to tell you about a man called Justin, don't you?

Justin's                    middle name is                    Michael.

---

Now you know what your peripheral vision can do, it's time to put it into practice in the real world.

---

**DO THIS**

- Go somewhere public where there are other people, like a park, a coffee shop or a pub.

- Sit somewhere and look straight ahead of you. Be careful not to stare at people. You don't want them thinking you're weird.

- As you look straight ahead, what can you see around you in your peripheral vision? Don't move your eyes, just notice what's around you.

- Take a 'guess' at who – or what – is behind you? Chances are your unconscious picked it up before you sat down.

---

As with anything else, the more you practise using your peripheral vision, the more aware you'll become of what's happening around you.

Now that you're able to pick up on the sort of stuff your unconscious brain usually does without you knowing, you can use this information to read other people's minds and get connection with them.

Getting connection is based on the principle that what your body does has a direct effect on your own mood. You can work out people's moods by looking (peripherally or otherwise) at what their body and face are doing, and then doing the same or something similar. That will have an effect on your own mood because of the connection between your body and your mood. Before we do that, here's a way of demonstrating the connection between your body and mood.

---

**DO THIS**

Next time you're out and about and walking somewhere, do the following:

- As you're walking, keep your head up and focus on the skyline, the rooftops, the tops of the trees, for a couple of minutes at least. Smile, even it's a false one. (Watch where you're going, though.)

- Now drop your head and hang it low. Look down at the pavement or the ground, slow your pace, put your hands in your pockets and hunch your shoulders, dragging your feet. Keep that going for a couple of minutes.

---

OK – how much did your mood change between the two? And all you did was change your physiology, right? Nobody told you to think about anything happy or sad, good or bad, something that cheers you up or something that gets you down, did they? No – it was just about your physiology.

So, if your physiology has a direct effect on your mood, then it follows that if you copy someone *else's* you'll go into a similar mood as them and you'll know how they're feeling. Right? That's another way to get inside someone's head. You can give this a go straight away.

---

**Remember This**

*Your mood is directly related to your physiology. Move your body about and you will move your mood. Read other people's moods by matching key parts of their physiology and noticing your own mood reflect theirs.*

---

**DO THIS**

Read someone's mood.

- Pick someone – anyone. It doesn't matter. Someone on a bus, in a shop, anywhere – someone you're not talking to.

- Do what they're doing, physically. If they lean back in their chair, do the same. Or if they cross their legs. Or fold their arms. Or scratch their nose. Or scratch their chin. Or stare into space. Or frown. Or smile. Or if they're walking in a certain way, or at a certain speed. Do the same.

- Check out how your own mood changes. Now you know more about how they're feeling.

---

You can prove this by simply going out and doing it. It will produce fantastic results.

Now that you can read people's moods, it's time to match

them so you can 'click' with them or get connection. Matching moods is easy. Once you've read someone's mood, stop for a second – and give the mood that you're reading its name. For example, *bored, happy, sad, curious, enthusiastic, annoyed, chilled out, nervous, excited*, etc. Now that your mood – and therefore the other person's mood – has a name, you've got everything you need to match it properly. It probably makes sense why you should match a positive mood, but you might be wondering why match a negative one, like *angry* or *annoyed*, for example. Go with it for now.

To match a mood properly, you need to know the secret of the great actors. What's the difference between a good actor and a great actor? What's the difference between Meryl Streep and Joey from *Friends*? Not Matt LeBlanc – Joey from *Friends*. Even though Meg Ryan delivered a Richter scale performance of seismic proportions when she sat across the table from Billy Crystal in *When Harry Met Sally*, we knew she was faking faking it, rather than authentically faking it. But what's Meryl Streep got over Meg Ryan and Joey? Well, at the last count, a whole stack of awards. She's been Oscar-nominated more times than anybody else. And she's one of a select group to have won all four major screen-acting awards (The Oscars, The Golden Globes, The Screen Actors Guild and BAFTA). Joey is not a member of that select group, in case you were wondering.

The Greeks, the ancient ones – not the modern ones – liked to amuse themselves with a bit of theatre. As you know, some of their performances were tragedies. Greek actors hid their faces behind a decorated mask, which had a fixed facial expression reflecting the personality of the character they were playing. The Greek word for this mask was *persona*. That's how the Greeks portrayed their persona on stage. It was all on the outside, on the surface. Joey would have fitted in well. Meryl Streep does things differently.

Meryl says that: 'If I'm not confident I can play the character perfectly, I won't even try.'

In the movie *Mamma Mia!*, her co-star Pierce Brosnan said he was stunned by her method acting in one scene when she got carried away and went to rip off his shirt: 'We were all dancing and enjoying the water and she got very happy. I was thinking "Should I do the same for her?"'. Why break the habit of a lifetime, 007?

When she starred in the Oscar-winning *Sophie's Choice*, she learned Polish for her role as a Polish Jew. She spoke the language so well that the Polish locals watching her filming the movie thought it was her first language.

Method actors do things differently. Daniel Day Lewis, Robert De Niro, Tom Hanks, Robin Williams, Al Pacino and Jane Fonda are method actors, too. They remember a time when they really felt the emotion that they want to portray. They remember not just the emotion but the situation – the *scene* from their life, if you like – that triggered that emotion. That means remembering specifically how they *felt* at the time, what they *saw* at the time, what they *heard* at the time – and, in some cases, what they *smelt* and *tasted* at the time. Only by bringing back the experience via their separate senses can they make it like a real-life experience again so they can give a real-life performance to the camera. It isn't pretending, faking or BSing. And it's certainly not acting. Apparently the secret of how Christopher Walken was so convincing in the Russian roulette scene in *The Deerhunter* was by recalling being sent to summer camp by his parents – an experience he hated. He says he felt betrayed, ostracized and alone – which he felt his character was experiencing in that moment in the film.

Do you want to learn how to do what Meryl Streep does? Do you want to be able to select the right mood for yourself? Do you want to match other people's? Once you're in the same mood, you'll get connection. You'll both feel like you've 'clicked'. Once you've done that you can then move that person into a mood you want them to be in so you can get what you want.

---

**DO THIS**

Changing someone's mood.

1. **Pick someone to read.** Just make sure at this stage that they're nice and detached, like your drycleaner, local shopkeeper, or supermarket checkout assistant. To put it another way, this means that you must *not* choose your husband, wife, boyfriend, girlfriend, mistress, sugar daddy, dominatrix, therapist, relatives, children or pet. This is only while you're practising. You'll be able to do it with anyone once you've got to the end of this book.

2. **Read them.** You know how to do this – using your body.

3. **Give their mood a name.** For example, 'happy', 'sad', 'nonplussed'.

4. **Reinforce the mood.** Using your internal dialogue (see pages 19–23), repeat the name of the mood over and over again in your head. Make sure your internal dialogue is speaking in a way that matches the mood you're now going into. Add your memories of a time you experienced that mood yourself. Get back the pictures that you saw at the time, the sounds you heard at the time and the emotion you felt at the time. Throw in some smells and tastes if you have them. Really go into the mood. Do a Meryl!

5. **Approach the person, maintaining the mood.** Talk to them normally, still maintaining the mood, until you're sure you're both 'in the same place' mood-wise.

6. **Keep going until you 'get connection' (see chapter 9) so you can change their mood.** You'll know once you've connected. You'll just feel it. It's a bit like that gut feeling you get when things are going well. You'll click. Now change their mood to a mood you *want them to be in* by gradually going into that mood yourself. Focus on gradually changing your gestures, your physiology, your smile. As you know, this will change your mood inside. Read their mood as it changes with yours. You've now got connection. If not, keep going until you have, or stop and try this exercise with someone else. Nothing is foolproof, remember, and you don't want to be one of those *how-to-achieve-exactly-the-opposite-of-what-this-book-is-intended-to-achieve*-type people.

Bingo, you've just influenced another person on an unconscious level using your non-verbal communication rather than words. Clever eh?

Guess what, you can get connection with more than one person at a time – even with a large group of people (they tend to fall into the same mood as each other – so match one mood and the rest will follow). You can even do it from across the road with a complete stranger that you've never spoken to in your life and never will. In fact, you have done already. You just didn't know.

You're walking along the road or through a doorway and someone else is coming the other way towards you. You step to one side to get by. They go the same way. You step the other way to get by. They do the same. It always happens with someone you've seen in advance, peripherally and often unconsciously. Like the way Tony saw those people behind him without thinking he'd seen them. They've usually been walking towards you – and your unconscious has 'got connection' with them without you realizing. It never happens with people who come at you from right angles and then turn in your direction at the last minute, does it?

Once you've got connection with someone, you'll find that you tend to come across in the right way automatically. You'll feel like you're getting on with each other and that you're 'clicking'. You won't even need to think much – you'll just find yourself doing and saying the right thing.

Without connection, you could get a slap in the face. I have had my face slapped a few times in my life. Here's why. It's all about kissing. Picture this.

---

**ALERT!** *How to achieve exactly the opposite of what this book is intended to achieve –*

There is a difference between matching and mirroring. You can match aspects of people's movements very subtly without being obvious. Don't copy people precisely (that's called 'mirroring' – and will have you making a fool of yourself).

---

I'm in a bar having a glass of wine with someone I quite fancy. Red? White? You choose, it's your picture. Bear in mind I don't know this person that well. In fact, it's the first time we've been out together. Things seem to be going well and we're getting on fine.

A few more glasses, a bit more chat, one more glass and I'm ready to move in. At least I think I am. I check with my internal dialogue. Yep. It's cheering away on the sideline.

'Go for it,' it says, 'you're definitely in there. I reckon she definitely likes you. High five!'

'OK,' I think, 'I just caught the way she smiled at me. That must mean I'm in. She's even twiddling her hair. She must be thinking the same thing.'

So, big deep breath, the next bit seems to happen in slow motion. In fact, it did in a way, because it lasted until I learned all this stuff.

I look into her eyes. I lean in, I lean in . . .

Where is she? She's not where she's meant to be. Oh God. She's sitting back in her chair. She's trying to pretend she hasn't noticed. I can't pretend. How do I get out of this? My face is practically in her drink. Shall I pretend I saw a fly in her glass and was attempting to remove it with my mouth?

Oh God.

These days I don't bother with too much thinking. Thinking is not all it's cracked up to be. I just make sure I get connection. Somehow, I now seem to know when the time is right. We find ourselves leaning in at exactly the same time, as if we both know automatically at the same time. You know what I mean.

Surprisingly often, getting connection is all you need to get what you want. Once you know – once you feel – you've got connection, just suggest what you want – or what you want the person to do – and see what happens.

It will save you the embarrassment of having to pretend you're rescuing insects from glasses of wine with your mouth. It almost always gets people to feel like they've clicked with you. It also gets them to like you (usually). Get in the habit of getting connection, in the way you've been reading, all the time with other people. You tend to do this naturally anyway. In fact, if human beings spend long enough together, they will eventually get connection automatically and unconsciously, which in turn makes them cooperate with

> ### Remember This
> *Once you find yourself going into their mood, maintain and reinforce it using your internal dialogue (see pages 19–23). Then gradually start to change your own mood, your own gestures, smile and so on and watch them come with you. When they do, you'll see that you've 'got connection'. You'll feel it, too. If not, just keep matching until you do.*

each other. It's a pack mentality and goes back to our caveman days. But now you know how to get connection quickly and consciously, you'll start getting much more of what you want.

Getting connection is your default position. It's the everyday version of getting what you want. Getting connection gets people to cooperate with you. There are no limits to it. If someone's in a bad mood or a negative frame of mind, you now know how to match their bad mood and then gently lead them out of it. If you're having a row, you now know how to end it. Match the person's angry mood and then gradually cheer them up. Same applies if they're sad, depressed, unhelpful, stressed, helpless or desperate. The more you do this, the better you get, until you do it without even thinking. Until it has become a new autopilot (see pages 41–46). It works better than just smiling and saying 'Cheer up' or something.

---

### DO THIS

This is what I used to do to get served in a busy bar. I would stand on the rail that runs along the floor on the customer side of the bar. I'd stick out my arm, waving money with my mouth open and a hopeful expression on my face saying 'Pick me – I'm next.' I always thought the bar staff went out of their way to avoid me.

This is what I do now.

1. Choose your barman from afar and stick to him. Don't change. If you do, you'll confuse everything. Including yourself. Confusion might well lead to learning most of the time but it doesn't lead to fast service.

2. Read his mood. You know how to do this.

3. Match his mood. Properly. Even if he's stressed – be stressed! Don't fake. Be like Meryl.

4. Reinforce your own matching mood, and wait for connection.

5. Order drinks.

6. Keep this to yourself, otherwise everyone'll be doing it.

We've covered quite a bit now – and most of it has gone in both consciously and unconsciously (by far the best way to learn new stuff). Think about what you can do now, that you couldn't do before you picked up this book. Think about all the autopilots you weren't aware of, all the information people were giving off that you weren't consciously picking up on, all the people in your life who you thought had the upper hand. The more you do it, the better you get. The better you get, the more you get. And you do want more, don't you?

Sometimes you'll just know that getting connection is not going to work for a particular person or situation. You'll know that the person just isn't prepared to cooperate with you. This is usually when there's a major rulebook clash (see chapter 4). If you're like me and you're naturally quite a nice person, and you like to do the right thing by others, then you need the following chapters even more.

I shouldn't really tell you this yet. When getting connection doesn't work, you need to tip the balance of power in your favour, take the lead, be in charge, make it hard for them to say no to you.

Don't be shy. Everyone's wearing that T-shirt, remember. You believe – you know, in fact – they can be persuaded again. Again, you just need to choose the right way. So, if connection hasn't worked, read on. No more Mr Nice Guy, it's kill or be killed. Dog eat dog. First among equals. Survival of . . . the most adaptable.

# Here's the end again

Recognize this? How much do you know already?

- Some of what you want is in your own hands. A lot is in the hands of other people. This book is about how you get those things that you want.

- In today's world, getting what you want means constantly adapting your behaviour to fit each situation.

- Thinking is made up of what you see, hear, feel and say to yourself inside your head. To get what you want, you need to ensure the other person is seeing, hearing, feeling and saying to themselves what you want them to.

- You have a specific set of principles, beliefs or values that are different from everyone else's. They are your codes and they determine how you think and behave. One of the obvious ways of not getting what you want is to assume that other people's codes are the same as yours.

- Getting what you want takes a bit of preparation and

thought. Decide exactly what you want before you even begin to go about getting it.

- Everyone has been persuaded before. Most people can be persuaded again. Sometimes they can't be persuaded at all. But then there's always someone else you can persuade if that turns out to be the case.

- The best way to persuade somebody is through their unconscious, or subconscious.

- Sometimes you need to be on the same wavelength as the other person to get what you want. At other times you need to be on different wavelengths.

- To get what you want, you need to work out what the other person wants first.

- Playing the celebrity is the most effective way of getting what you want.

- Getting personal or getting impersonal can get you what you want, depending on the situation.

- Everyone likes credit. Give people some – but not too much.

- People will often keep their word if you make them feel they owe you.

- The words you choose, and the way you say them, can persuade people without them realizing.

- Be ready for your enemies and be prepared to stop them getting what they want.

# 10

# Make it Hard to Say No

You might recognize these first few paragraphs. You've read them before, earlier on. But it's so important, that they're in here again. They're especially important when you want to make it hard for people to say no to you.

To get what you want – you strike first. Here's why. If you let others strike first, they might get what they want instead and you might not get what you want at all. This means making the first move, preparing for the conversation in a particular way. It means taking the lead, thinking first, and acting first. If you start second, you'll probably come second, or third. It would be an uphill struggle from that moment to get what you want. You'd be on the back foot. You could still get what you want from that position but you'd need to work twice as hard. So strike first.

Whatever you do and say in the first five seconds of meeting somebody are the most important things you'll probably ever do and say to them. You know that already. First impressions count. Knowing what you know about their unconscious and their autopilots (see pages 41–46), what do you think their unconscious mind is going to make of you if you strike first and get the upper hand straight away? What message does their unconscious get about you? You know there are two parts of you so now let's look at the two parts of me. Imagine we're at a meeting. Here's what happens to me – in both my conscious and my unconscious – if you strike first at that meeting.

What's going on in my conscious mind will look like this.

*And what's going on in my unconscious mind will look like this.*

You: Hi, Mark and Scott? I've only got 15 minutes, so for the sake of quickness, I've put together a quick agenda of points I want to cover.

Me: Hi, good to meet you. That's fine. Fire away.

*Uh-oh. What the \*\*\*\* just happened? What am I going to have for dinner tonight ? I've just gone blank. What are we supposed to be talking about? It wasn't dinner. This person doesn't mess around. Better stop thinking about my dinner and read these agenda points so that I've got some answers ready. This person's in charge of this conversation. I'm right on the back foot here and I might look like a right dickhead if I'm not on the ball. Right – focus. I'd better go along with this. Fishfingers!*

Except all that unconscious thought takes place in approximately 54.75 nanoseconds. Roughly the same amount of time it takes for a slice of buttered toast to fall face-down on the kitchen floor if you drop it.

Here's why first impressions count. It's called the primacy effect. The primacy effect – that first impression – lodges in your mind, even if later impressions contradict it. So much so, that you will overlook most information that comes later and stick with what you thought at first. So, if your unconscious thinks someone's in charge because they've taken the lead at first, it will always think they're in charge, whether they continue to be in charge or not. As humans have evolved, we have had to develop a reliable 'first impression' system to survive. And it is reliable. Otherwise you wouldn't be here. None of us would.

So now we've got the first thing out of the way, this section is about getting other people to say yes to you. You do that by making it hard for them to say no. You reduce their options and stack the odds in your favour by persuading them at an unconscious level to give you what you want. Appealing to people's autopilots (see pages 41–46) in this way is far more effective than just going for a straight, and conscious, 'yes'. The best way to persuade someone is when they're not aware you're trying to persuade them. That's when you catch them with their barriers down and their autopilots visible for you to use to your advantage.

In this part of the book, you're going to get a full set of techniques to choose from. Just remember that whichever one – or two or three or more – you choose at any time, you strike first. That means getting in before the other person.

There will be words and phrases that have a psychologically persuasive effect on people. I'm also going to show how celebrities get what they want, and how you can learn from them. Then we'll talk about when it's good to be personal with people and when it's better to distance yourself to get what you want. Giving credit is another way of persuading people, as long as you give just the right amount. And, once someone has agreed to give you what you want, it's important that you know how to hold them to what they've promised.

Finally, for when you become really good, you learn how to break connection (once you've got it), which can sometimes be the key to getting what you want.

Each technique is specifically designed and some techniques are better in certain situations. If you find you're not getting anywhere with the technique you've chosen, just adapt – and do another one. It's a bit like evolution on fast forward – you do it really quickly. The result is the same: success.

Getting what you want can be summed up like this. Once you've made it hard for people to say no, they usually say yes instead. Some people call it getting compliance.

There are good examples of this everywhere. Let's start with an obvious one – the army, and how difficult it makes it for people to say no. It might be assumed that if you don't do as you're told by your senior officers, you might die, right? Well, yes, maybe. But what if you think your way of not dying is better than your commanding officer's idea of how not to die? Then you wouldn't do as you're told, would you? But soldiers do. (I'm struggling to get inside the head of a soldier, to be honest. I'm a bit of a wuss. If I really need to die, I'd rather it was in my own bed after a nice cup of cocoa and a nap.)

Remember my mate Mark? The one with the flip flops who was made redundant when the recession came (see pages 5–8)? He had a few mates who'd joined the army straight from school. One was based in Belize, another one was in Brüggen in Germany, and another was in Cyprus. They loved it. When they came home on leave they talked about beer, guns, silicon versus real, beaches, cans, jumping in and out of bushes surprising people, mates, women and beer.

When Mark decided to follow his mates and join up he found that he had no real problems with the aptitude tests. He was pretty fit. He played a lot of sport, which got him a one-way ticket to the barracks.

He arrived by train from Reading at 0900 hours one Sunday morning in his civvies. His internal dialogue had talked about what to wear on his first day – and he'd seen pictures in his mind's eye of men in smart uniforms. So he made a real effort. He'd never looked smarter. He'd put on a pair of jeans, shoes and a short-sleeved shirt. The shell necklace was still there, clinging to his neck like a barnacle. What do you mean, that's not smart? Rulebooks remember; everyone's is different.

Mark went to the quartermaster's store to get his kit. He was waiting in the queue for his uniform when a warrant officer approached him and said hello. (I might need to remind you at this point, before I go on, that Mark had been used to free mineral water and bacon sandwiches at breakfast meetings, free beer on a Friday, TV in the office – and long lunch hours.) Mark was a friendly bloke. He winked and smiled at the warrant officer – 'All right?!'

Before he joined up, Mark had imagined that he would be in the army for a bit more than five minutes before the outbreak of World War Three. I'm told that according to records, the loudest noise you can ever experience on earth is the sound of a space shuttle lifting off. Mark assures me, with great authority, that the space shuttle is not deserving of this title while there is still blood flowing through the veins of one Warrant Officer Billy 'Beasting' Smith.

If you want a rough idea of the sheer volume of noise that

came out of Warrant Officer Smith's bombastic mouth, I want you to imagine you're at a rock concert in the front row. At each side of the stage there is a speaker roughly the size of Greater London.

The sound that emanated from under Warrant Officer Billy Smith's half-kilo moustache was not only as loud as those speakers, it was the stereo type of sound that passes straight through your body, turning your vital organs into a pulp. 'Say "All right?"again and you'll be doing PT until you puke your guts up and then, when you can't puke any more, you'll be doing more PT until you puke some more. And just when you're starting to wish you could die for it to stop, I'm going to stamp my boot on your scrawny neck not quite hard enough to kill you but more than enough to make you a vegetable before you've got a chance to write home to Mummy asking her to come and collect you. Do I make myself clear?'

'And what the **** is that round your neck?'

That was the first time that Warrant Officer Smith and Mark met. Smith was quick in making it hard for Mark to say no to him, as you've just seen. Of course, Smith wasn't going to stamp on Mark's neck. He just needed Mark making pictures of his boot doing that (like you did) to put him in a compliant frame of mind. From that moment, Mark was ready – and willing – to give Warrant Officer Smith what he wanted.

The military specialize in getting people to do as they're told. In some ways they are so good at this that troops would rather face the enemy – and certain death – than get on the wrong side of their commanding officers. Everyone knows the rules and – unlike in the real world – the rules are the same for everyone.

The rules have been there since Mark's shell necklace was sitting at the bottom of the sea.

Everyone also knows the consequences of breaking those rules. Everyone does as they are told. The military has been doing human compliance very well for thousands of years. Freedom of thought, a bubbly personality, creativity workshops, Tellytubby nicknames, signing emails with kisses, mind mapping, bean-bag brainstorms and thought showers have no place in a tank surrounded by machete-wielding militiamen with rocket-propelled grenades.

Learning how to get compliance plays a big part in your campaign strategy to get what you want. To learn how to do it yourself, you need to learn from the experts.

*Inside the army camp is a huge contrast to your life in the outside world. A deliberate shock to the system. A visual punch in the mouth – telling you this place is different. The rules of the outside world no longer apply. There is no room for colour or personality or being an individual. No indulgence, no luxury, no enjoyment – not as you know it. Not a bottle of Evian in sight. You won't need to think about what to wear in the morning any more. In fact, you won't need to think about very much at all.*

This is why you stick to the rules. Why it's hard for you to say no. This is why you comply. And how the military gets what it wants.

Now stop reading.

OK you can start reading again now.

Who else is good at making it hard to say no? My old manager always held meetings in his own office and made me close the door behind me. We didn't have to wear uniforms at that place but there were rules about what you could wear. I once worked at a place where they didn't allow you to leave the building all day. They even provided you with free food to keep you there. The staff canteen was in the basement.

I had to show an ID pass to get past reception at work. And you had to carry your magnetic security fob around with you at all times because you needed to get through certain doors.

You don't have to copy the army. There's a series of making-it-hard-to-say-no techniques coming up so you can win compliance from other people in your everyday life. And you won't have to wield a gun, make people wear a uniform or grow a moustache.

# 11

# Persuasion Technique Number 2: Psychologically Speaking

**ALERT!** *How to achieve exactly the opposite of what this book is intended to achieve –*

Huge alert. What you're about to know is either fantastically brilliant or really bad. If you do it well, no one will notice. If you do it badly, you will lose. Doing it well means you *must* have connection first and you've got to be yourself while you're doing it. Choose the phrases you can imagine yourself saying, or might normally say anyway. Avoid the ones that aren't 'you'.

Once you've got connection (see chapter 9), you can stack the odds in your favour by what you do with your words. It's not just what you say, it's how you say it. There are ways of using your words to exert a psychological effect on another person's unconscious mind to make it hard to say no, make them more likely to agree with you, and give you what you want. As I hope you've already read, you must have connection before you do this and you've got to do it realistically and credibly.

The psychology of what you're about to know is rooted in hypnosis, but you won't be doing any hypnosis. The difference between using it hypnotically and non-hypnotically is when you put someone in a trance you can say what you like to them. They won't notice. But they will if you haven't put them in a trance! People often go wrong using this type of language because they think it's a form of superpower and they suddenly fancy themselves as some kind of Jedi knight. The fact that you are *not* putting people into a hypnotic trance first means you need to pay attention to how you come across. If not, you'll have them running screaming for the hills. Be aware of yourself and be yourself. Otherwise you won't get what you want.

Read through these and pick out the phrases you think will suit you best. (Ignore the ones you wouldn't say.) You can use these anywhere. Use them to persuade people once you've got connection – or you can use them to 'max out' any of the techniques that are coming later.

**State the obvious:** If you want someone to think something is obvious, just say it is. Like this: *We both know* it'll be worth it once we've been. *You probably know this already, but* we offer the best deals on the market. *Obviously* I'm going to need a discount if it's been on display in the shop.

**The question that's not really a question:** You know all about these already, don't you. If you want to persuade someone's unconscious to agree with you – just say what you want it to agree with and then put a question at the end. It's easy, isn't it. Probably time for another drink, isn't it. My plane's about to leave; it's OK if I jump the queue, isn't it. Warning: this is good for everyday stuff. Obviously it can't be relied upon to get people to marry you, sleep with you or give you all their money, can it.

By the way, make sure your intonation goes down at the end of your question and not up like a real question – otherwise you invite the person to say no. In case you've been wondering, that's why we've deliberately left out some of the question marks whenever we've used this device in this book, haven't we. It's to make sure your internal dialogue's intonation goes down when you read it, and not up – like a question.

**Get them saying yes:** You probably know this already but you've just learned one way, haven't you.

Here's another way: Say 'Let's' – and follow it with what you want to do – 'Let's go for a walk', or 'Let's have another drink' or 'Let's go to my place.' This is a command in disguise. Compare it with 'Shall we go for a walk?' or 'Shall we have another drink?' or 'Shall we go to my place?', which makes it easy for them to say no.

The more you can get someone saying 'Yes', the more likely they are to keep saying yes. By getting them to say 'Yes' several times in succession, you train their mind to be compliant. Think of it like this: their mind goes into a 'Yes' kind of mood. So save the thing you really want until last, once they've said yes a few times.

**This or that:** 'Can I get you a cocktail while you're waiting, or would you just like a glass of wine?' said the waiter. The reason it worked was because he gave me two options – both of which were good for him. The only choice he gave me was between a cocktail and wine. Not whether I wanted a drink or not. You know this already in some forms. A good waiter will ask you – before even checking whether you want wine or water – 'Red or white, sir?', 'Sparkling or still?' But please don't try 'My place or yours?' It's been done to death. This works most effectively in combination with the 'I'm a celebrity' principle later in the book.

**Predict the future:** 'You'll love this one.' Just tell them how you want them to react to something by saying that's how they *will* react. 'I know this will be right up your street.' 'I know you're going to want to do this again.' 'Wait until you hear what I've got to tell you; I know you're going to be impressed.'

**Leaps of logic:** You've read this far so you already know how to get what you want. You know all about people's unconscious autopilots; that means you're a master of persuasion. Use the word 'so' or the phrase 'that must mean' to create a link between two concepts that may or may not be there. The first concept is always true. The second one – the one you link it to – is what you want them to agree to.

For example, you're reading this book (true) so you must be enjoying it (probably true and I certainly want it to be). Or 'We've been together for three months now, so of course I'm committed to this relationship.' Or 'I've been with this company for three years and demonstrated my loyalty; that must mean it's time for us to sit down and talk about my position and my salary. When's a good time?'

**Command and command:** 'Think about it and give me a call.' It's the first command you really want them to obey, but if you immediately follow it with another command that you know they'd agree with anyway, the person will only 'hear' the second one and will usually obey the first one without question. 'It's late and you're tired. Take the rubbish out and come to bed early.' Or 'Come for a drink and tell me about it . . .'

**I shouldn't really tell you this but . . .** This creates loyalty and trust. It makes people feel special. It also gently encourages them at an unconscious level to treat you as a special case – and draw you into their confidence. 'But obviously this is between these four walls. Just between you and me.' Or, 'I'll let you into a secret . . .'

**But:** 'He's always late for work but he's good at his job.' 'He's good at his job but he's always late for work.' What's the difference between these two statements? Whatever comes after the 'but' is the one you take most notice of – the point you really want to make. Or, 'I know I haven't got much experience in this field, but I do have a proven track record in adapting quickly to new environments.' Or, 'You're a nice guy but you're not my type.' Or 'I really like you, but I'm happy being single at the moment.' Using 'but' like this 'hides' the point you really want to make so you make it much more subtly.

**The ideal question:** 'What do you want ideally?' Or 'What are you looking for ideally?' Or 'What ideally do you want to happen?' Or 'What's the ideal outcome?' Or make up your own: as long as it contains the word 'ideal' or 'ideally', and is about what they want, it doesn't really matter how you ask it. The power of this question is massive. It does all kinds of things:

- It gets people to tell you the truth about what they want.

- It gets them away from thinking about what they *don't* want.

- The word 'ideal' or 'ideally' gets them to create pictures in their mind of things that are perfect for them, rather than merely what they think might be possible. Seeing these pictures of perfect things has an enormous effect on their mood, as you can imagine.

- It gives you all the information you need to be able to influence them. Once you've got this information – and more importantly – the very *words* they used when giving it to you, you must then start using those precise words back to them *because they perfectly match their perfect pictures*. And why would you want to mess with their perfect pictures? They're ideal, remember. And using your own words – however similar the meanings you *think* they have – will more than likely mess up that ideal for them.

To see what I mean, do this:

## DO THIS

I'll say something, and you make a note in your mind of what you see when I say it.

*A boat.*
What did you see? I saw a small sailing dinghy, and a passenger ferry. What did you see? The same, or something different? Let's do another one.

*A lot of money.*
What did you see? I saw lots of banknotes, about a thousand pounds. I saw a stack of gold coins, all piled up on top of each other.

*A nice house.*
What did you see? I saw a smart town house with three floors and an ultra-modern kitchen with all mod cons. I saw a Californian-style beachfront pad.

You see, the same words make different pictures in different people's minds. That's why you need to use *their* words to match *their* pictures once they've answered your ideal question.

If you work in sales or you need to 'sell' yourself in any situation – like a job interview or if you run your own company, this is a very good way of coming across to people in the way they like. Of course, you'll have done all the other obvious stuff first, like some research on who you'll be seeing, updated your CV, made sure you've dressed appropriately and so on.

This is for when you're finally in the room with them and you want to make it hard to say no.

If you ask the ideal question at a job interview 'So, ideally, what's the ideal candidate you're looking for?' or 'Who would be your ideal candidate?', the interviewer will probably answer you with a description of the picture in their mind's eye of their perfect candidate. All you need to do is make sure you come back at them *as* that candidate, using the very words that they've used, and tailoring your answers to fit that description. Or, if you're hitting on someone, just say (after you've got connection of course – see chapter 9) 'So tell me about your ideal (man or woman) then.' Then just shut up and listen to the answer. Pick out the bits that apply to you and focus on delivering them – and play down the bits about you that don't fit that description.

If your job involves getting people to 'buy into' you whatsoever – and it does, when you think about it, whatever you do! – just ask the ideal question instead of endlessly trying to second-guess people. One ideal question will usually get someone to tell you everything you need to know.

Try it and see. And once they've begun answering, you keep quiet and let them talk. Even if they pause as they think – just stay quiet. They won't notice. Don't interrupt or try to finish their sentence. They'll give you all the info you need – and most of the good stuff will come after they've paused to think. So shut up.

**Don't say 'yes' unless you mean it . . .** This strengthens commitment. Say this before they agree to what you want from them. If they do end up agreeing to your demands, it makes it difficult for them to back out. It also works if you say 'Don't decide now unless you're sure.'

**Say it without saying it:** There are a few ways of making a point – and making pictures in the other person's mind – without looking like you're making them. 'I can't be the one to tell you to ditch him – it's up to you to decide.' 'I'm not going to be the one to say I told you so.' 'I don't even want to think about the amount of pressure you must be under at the moment.' 'I don't want you to worry about me; I'll be fine on my own.' All you do is make the point by saying you're not making it. You can also issue commands by telling people not to do what you want them to do. 'Don't worry about paying me back!'

**Use quotes:** If I thought you were drifting off and I wanted to get you to pay attention, I could deliver that command 'under the radar' with this technique: I could tell you that I went out for a drink with a friend of mine the other day. I could tell you that I was preoccupied, that she kept talking to me but that I was drifting in and out of the conversation – until she lost her cool and suddenly shouted 'Will you pay attention to me, please!'

Or try it like this. If you're with someone who's down in the dumps, you might want to talk about a time when you were really upset and '(someone) said to you "Come on, snap out of it – it's gone on long enough now and it's time to move on."'

**Do it without quotes:** An old colleague of mine does the same thing but without using quotes. So do a lot of politicians. Just attribute a comment or behaviour to someone else – to send unconscious messages. All the experts say it's a lot easier to send unconscious messages than people think.

**Yes means no:** 'I could . . . if you like?' This is a way of offering to do something you don't really want to do. For example, 'I could drive, if you like?' 'I could do that, if you like?' 'I could stay late, if you like?' Unlike the question that's not really a question (see page 115), make sure your intonation goes up at the end of it (not down) – so that you persuade them unconsciously that they need to say no to you. And make sure you say 'I could' and not 'I can . . .' or 'I will . . .'

**It's not important, but it is really:** 'I know you won't care about this, but it really worries me how unhealthy your lifestyle is.' 'You might not care about this, but your deodorant wears off a bit too soon in the day. Have you thought about keeping a spare in your desk?' 'You may not think it's important, but I have seen him having lunch with the same woman three times in the last two weeks.' This is the one to use if you want to deliver information that the other person might not like, or may not want to hear.

**A polite way to say 'Shut up and listen to me':** For example, 'I don't know if you understand how hard it is for me to do a full day's work and still come home and feed the kids.' Or, 'I don't know if you can see how long I've been putting up with this.' Or, 'I don't know if you realize how long I've been waiting for my main course.' Or if you want to get really heavy, 'I'm not sure if you realize how unattractive I'm feeling at the moment.'

**The meeting before the meeting:** The next time you're due to have a conversation with one or more people you want to influence, stop first and think about what exactly you want from them. This could be a meeting at work, a discussion with a friend or someone at home. It could even be one of your friends who keeps ignoring all your best advice and is making the same mistake over and over again. Someone you want to influence for what you consider to be a good reason.

Never formally announce the beginning of the meeting or conversation. Just start to make your points informally. If you do need to announce formally that a discussion has started, make sure you've made all your points informally before that. This also works at the end of the discussion. Once it's been formally closed, it's a great time to make any points you didn't make before it started.

Here's why this works. As soon as a meeting or discussion is announced or opened, people go into meeting/discussion 'mode'. That means the unconscious part of their brain is 'ready for you'. It knows that you will try to persuade it to do things it doesn't necessarily want to do. The guard goes up and you need to work ten times as hard to get what you want.

I call it the meeting before the meeting. Or the discussion before the discussion. Or the meeting after the meeting. Or the discussion after the discussion. It's also the difference that makes the difference. Try it and see.

While we're talking about words, here's a quick tangent. Do you know why 'retail therapy' is called retail therapy? The term was deliberately coined by a bunch of clever marketing people. The two words 'retail' and 'therapy'. What do they mean to you? Let's take the first word – 'retail'. Pretty dry word, isn't it? What does it conjure up in your mind when you say it? A retail park, maybe? Retail outlets? Shop assistants who would rather be somewhere else? Trying to get a refund? (Later on, there's a great technique for getting refunds, by the way. You'll love it.)

Now let's take the word 'therapy'. No – not that therapy when you have to lie on a couch and talk to a strange man with a German accent and bear all. I'm talking about the nice, pleasant kind of therapy, like aromatherapy, massage therapy, seaweed wraps, steam rooms, sea salt scrubs and other sensuous soothing sensations.

Some people really know how to use the right words to make you feel good. Well, to make you feel, full stop, as a matter of fact. How do you feel about the idea of that kind of therapy? It's a psychological fact that shopping does make you feel better, at least for a short while, after you've maxed out your plastic and worn yourself out walking round the shops. But if I want you to shop a lot, I would much rather have you associate it with feeling good rather than spending money.

Here's the point of that tangent: words can have positive or negative connotations. By choosing your words carefully, you can create good or bad associations in someone's mind. That's hugely important when it comes to getting what you want.

# 12

# Persuasion Technique Number 3:
## I'm a Celebrity

'I'm a celebrity' means coming across like you're in charge, in authority, special, an expert, individual, in demand, busy, popular, one step ahead, or ever so slightly unapproachable so that people feel lucky to be in your company. It's also about looking good or looking the part. Using your celebrity is usually the most effective way of making it hard for people to say no. It's the technique if getting what you want is the most important thing to you, and you don't much care what people think.

You may or may not be a celebrity. Even if you are, you probably don't know everything about your celebrity. You may think that celebrities get what they want simply because they're celebrities? Wrong. The only differences between you and a celebrity are: many people recognize them but don't know them; they're probably richer than you, but not necessarily.

In short, they're rich and famous. But that doesn't automatically make them in charge, in authority, special, an expert, individual, in demand, busy, popular, one step ahead . . .

Celebrities get a lot of what they want because they have the confidence to behave in certain ways. Using the essence of celebrity is not just about who you are, it's also about what you do. What you do can get you what you want without you having to record a hit song, appear live on stage or host a prime-time TV show.

You need to go back to that T-shirt that everyone's wearing (see chapter 8) and remind yourself that everyone can be persuaded again. You can choose what you believe, remember. And that means you can also choose to believe in your own celebrity. Then, you take the essence of what it is to be in the public eye and adapt it for yourself. It's actually really simple. The power of celebrity has been around for eons. Let's start with how you can use your celebrity in the workplace, and move on to your private life after that.

Most of the time at work, you'll need to assert your celebrity at meetings. Meetings can happen formally around a table, by chance in a corridor, in your boss's office, or over a coffee in a back room. I'll start with the more formal version, the one that has an agenda, a big table and all the other props. All of this gets much easier as soon as you've done it once. As you read through these for the first time, can you please tell your internal dialogue (see pages 19–23) to be quiet. It may begin saying in your head, 'I can't. I couldn't. I wouldn't have the guts. What would people think of me? That's not me.' That kind of thing. But ignore it. Using your celebrity breaks down into four areas:

- Being on your territory

- Being in demand

- Looking the part

- Standing out from the crowd.

## Be on your territory

Whenever possible, arrange to meet on your own territory. Meet on neutral territory if you must. But avoid their territory when you can.

Say hi to Sharon. Sharon lives in a lovely house. It's a converted village hall, or something like that, but it's very pleasant. Expensive, too. Granite worktops in the kitchen, big glass extension for a dining room and extra sitting room. Plus the obligatory room at the front of the house that nobody does much with but estate agents for some reason say is essential. It all cost Sharon a lot. But that didn't matter at the time because she was earning a massive salary. She had a really good job with a perfect life/work balance. She was often allowed to work from home. Some people would call that a licence to be lazy but her boss didn't. He thought it made sound business sense. Sharon also had a daughter. Her husband had a job, too, but wasn't nearly as successful. Sharon was the breadwinner. She was the boss. Everyone thought highly of her – at work and at home. Sharon didn't have to work that hard to earn her money. She was brilliant at getting what she wanted.

Sharon liked showing off her nice house. She had plenty of

room, spare bedrooms, a big garden and another one of those strange rooms upstairs that nobody uses but estate agents say are essential. There were stainless-steel gadgets everywhere. She loved it when people came over. Friends stayed the night. Colleagues came for meetings over coffee but often ended up staying for dinner. Sharon's husband was a brilliant cook. All of this made it hard to say no to Sharon.

My rulebook (see chapter 4) would tell me that Sharon is a great host. She's hospitable and she likes looking after her guests. Another rulebook would say that's all true but she's also lazy because everyone has to go to her house. Sharon never goes to anyone else's.

Her rulebook went like this: she went out of her way to get people onto her turf, her territory. If Sharon gets you to her house to get what she wants from you, how hard is it to say no? Bearing in mind you're sitting on her sofa, in her garden, around her dinner table, or about to sleep in one of her guest beds, having eaten her food and drunk her wine and coffee? How much easier is it to say no to Sharon if you're in a coffee shop, in an open-plan office, on the phone, or at your own house?

## Be in demand

Being in demand is about not being available all the time. You need to look busy and make it difficult for people to tie you down. Make sure you're not always at your desk and if people try to grab a quick chat, tell them you haven't got time to speak to them right now.

Before a meeting starts, set a time for it to end – on your terms. Say something important has cropped up and you need to be gone by a certain time, earlier than the meeting was due to end originally. You won't be able to do this at every meeting, obviously. Use it every now and again. This works because people will feel they're taking up your time and that the time you do have is precious. It also means they'll be in a hurry to make their points before you leave. It puts them under pressure and disarms them. Think about when you're under pressure. You're not at your best. And if they *do* have any manipulation tactics up their sleeve, they won't feel there's time to use them. They'll be on the back foot.

Sharon was an expert at 'being in demand', too. As well as getting you to her house whenever she could, she also took a lot of phone calls and emails on her BlackBerry. Especially while you were talking to her. She was always very busy, you see. She was always sorry when she did it because she knew it was rude. But some people are so busy – and therefore so important – they can't help it. Aren't they?

Sharon treated her office like her own home. She received a lot of visitors there. You get why now. When she wasn't in her office, she was in meetings elsewhere – presumably because, on that occasion, she'd been unable to get people to her office.

Well, to be more precise, people *assumed* she was in meetings most of the time. That was what it said in her Outlook calendar and she was always hard to get hold of. Even on her mobile. Her PA always took calls on her behalf. Whether she was there or not.

It didn't matter, though. Most people would tell you she was brilliant at her job. Most people listened to most people. People do that a lot. Actually she was brilliant at her job, it was true. From as soon as she joined the company many years ago. Brilliant. It made it hard for people to say no to her. They remembered it for years and didn't notice if she was still doing a brilliant job. You remember the primacy effect (see pages 107–108). First impressions count – and people remember them, and act on them, for ages. It comes from your caveman instinct to survive.

If your first impression of a charging mammoth is that it looks dangerous – you'll remember that for next time and live to fight another day. You won't hang around to give the next mammoth the benefit of the doubt. If people's first impression of you is as someone with celebrity, they'll remember you as someone with celebrity. It will work in your favour for ages. That's why you strike first with it.

## Look the part

Think about what you're wearing. To assert your celebrity you need to dress one notch 'up' or 'better' than whoever you want to influence. In other words, if you know their style is casual, wear a suit. If you know they wear suits, wear a better suit. This goes for bags, briefcases, glasses, pens, shirts, man-bags and handbags, too. But make sure it's only one notch 'up'. So if the people you want to influence go to work in T-shirts and jeans, you wear a shirt, jeans and shoes if you're a man – or a skirt and shoes if you're a woman. Not a suit. This works because of the primacy effect that I mentioned earlier. First impressions count. Being one notch 'up' from someone sends a message to their unconscious that you are more successful than them and makes them likely to defer to you.

So, you've thought about what you're wearing beforehand. You know what you're going to say. And you're starting to get your head around what I'm a celebrity is all about. Stop saying yes! You've just said yes, in your mind, to me more than once. Getting people to say yes is easy. Check out how many times you've said yes today, and while you've been reading this book. The point is that if you're nodding, then the people you're nodding to are in authority because you're saying yes to them. In your meeting, you want everyone nodding and saying yes to you. But you need to control your own nodding. Hold your head still when you can and do something instead of nodding – like click your pen, twiddle with your pen, doodle, tap your feet, blink, clench your jaw, anything to satisfy your unconscious that you're doing something instead of nodding. Try to say 'Mmm' or 'OK' or 'Right' instead of 'Yes'. You must never imply that you agree 100 per cent with what's being said. Not while you're at the meeting, at least. This works because you're sending a message that you are not complying with them. Their unconscious will pick up that they haven't got compliance and they will be in a slight state of doubt. They'll keep trying to get connection with you (see chapter 9), which puts them on the back foot and you in charge.

## Stand out from the crowd

Set the agenda for any meetings in advance, or if you can't set it, make sure you set some of it. Even if that means sending an email ahead of a meeting, asking for your material to be included. Never let others set it all. If all else fails, suggest another agenda item at the meeting itself, preferably before the meeting starts. This sends an unconscious message to the others that you are at least an equal partner in the discussion. Failing to do so sends a message that they are in charge and not you.

When you get to the meeting, make sure you are last to sit down. Claim space on the table. Make sure the space you occupy on the table is bigger than anyone else's by putting your notepad, pen, mobile, glasses case, etc. down around you. Remember, I'm not talking about getting connection. We've done all that already. This is about your celebrity. If everyone's sitting down at the meeting, don't be shy of standing up. Be confident! It's easier than you might think. Especially when you use your internal dialogue (see pages 19–23) and pictures to tell yourself you're feeling confident by thinking of a time when you've been confident in the past. You can say you need to stretch your legs, or you need to stand up to think. Or you need to use a prop.

When you're really good at this, you won't feel the need to say anything at all. You'll simply stand up when you want to, to show your celebrity. Showing celebrity is a million times better than talking about it. Remember that. This works because you're a primate. You've probably seen this on nature pro-grammes. Primates operate in groups and recognize the leader of the pack. He's the one who stands tall, goes where he wants, sleeps with whom he wants and gets first pickings at meal-times. Taking up physical space like this sends a message to other primates – human or not, it doesn't matter – that you're the alpha male or female. It tells them you're in charge.

You don't show your celebrity by leaning forward and looking fascinated. To show their autopilots (see pages 41–46) that you're in charge, sit back. Cross your arms if you like, and your legs. This is one of the rare occasions when crossing your arms probably does send an unconscious signal of distance between you and other people *because you're doing it at the same time as sitting back and crossing your legs etc.* And yes, getting what you want sometimes means breaking connection. This works because you first get connection and then take it away. There's more on breaking connection later. It forces the others unconsciously to try to get connection back with you – and means they'll start to follow your lead. Watch them lean into you. Watch them try to get your attention and try to make eye contact with you and keep it. Every now and then you should give them their connection back – and then take it away again.

Question other people throughout the meeting. Make sure you frown from time to time and say 'I'm not sure I understand what you're saying. Just go back to the beginning and explain it to me again' (or a similar version of that question that is more 'you'). Ask this question even if you've understood every word they've said. And, whatever you do, don't apologize for not understanding. That would tell their autopilots that it's your fault for not understanding. This works because you tell their autopilots – without actually *saying so* – that it is in fact their fault for not explaining something properly.

If you're visiting another company or client, never sit down in reception; walk around looking inquisitive and interested.

Never sit down. Even if you're invited to sit down, say you're OK standing. Ask them if they'd mind getting you a drink, before they offer.

On the occasions Sharon did go into work, she always drove. Or was driven. As a female executive she was entitled to her own late-night taxi account to take her to her front door whenever she wanted. She never ever took public transport. What autopilots would kick off in the unconscious part of your brain if you met someone who never got public transport and made sure you knew it? What pictures might you see in your mind's eye? What might you think really quickly – and almost not notice yourself thinking it? Sharon knows this and she's made you think this and see those pictures deliberately. You're probably seeing her driving – or being driven – around in a very smart car. Remember, you're far more predictable than you like to think. You're thinking she's standing out from the crowd. She's rich, famous, successful, almost a celebrity. Public transport is for everyone else – not her. That must mean she's special in some way. A bit of a show-off, maybe. Even pretentious. But still a celebrity in some way. And special.

If your internal dialogue has already kicked off, fretting that you don't have the house, the kitchen, the office or the stainless steel, not to mention the driver, the executive title and the spare bedrooms you don't need – don't worry. Sharon didn't actually need all that to use her celebrity. You can use almost anything. There's a 'Do This' coming soon to help you with that.

So how many autopilots did Sharon fire off in your mind? In other words, how many assumptions did you make about her based on what she did or said? And, based on those assumptions that she deliberately put in place – being an expert on most people's autopilots as she is – how much authority did she have in people's minds? And over people's minds? She isn't a celebrity but read again the sections above on how she behaved to get what she wanted.

A quick word about numbers. Never be outnumbered. At least be equal. Have more on your side if you can. If you have to be in the minority and there's no choice – use everything in this section to get what you want.

Maybe you're not a high-flying executive and have no desire to be one. Maybe you don't need to go to meetings at work. Maybe you don't have even one stainless-steel kitchen gadget and maybe you can account for the purpose of every single room in your house. Maybe you're normal – like us – and like most people. Maybe you're not in a position of authority for you to use your celebrity at work. If so, it's time for you to come up with your own version. Think of how you want to use your celebrity to get something at work. And who you want to influence to get it.

---

**DO THIS**

- Do the normal thing – decide exactly what you want and who you want it from.

- What is your territory? Where is your territory? Is it your home, your place of work or your car? Your desk? Your favourite place – a place you know like the back of your hand – like a shop or a bar where you know the staff, a restaurant or coffee shop where you know other people? Is it somewhere else? Failing that, where is some neutral territory you can use? If it's neutral, make it yours. Make sure you know something about the place in advance, like where the toilets are, what's the best dish on the menu, etc. Claim some ownership of the place.

- What props can you use to be in demand? How can you play hard to get without it blowing up in your face? How can the person you need to influence feel fortunate to know you? How can you come across as busy in your spare time? How can you make it look as if your life is really packed with interesting stuff without actually telling people so? Using your flash new phone, for example, works much better than telling people you've got one. Or wearing your new designer top, being seen in your flash car, or going to a new club.

- How can you look the part? What do you have that gives you status? Mobile phone? Car? Bike? Clothes? Gadgets? Evidence of your past successes and/or current status? What reflects good aspects of your lifestyle? What else? What props can you use by association – for example, a friend with a nice car? Or a friend with a great job? People can be props, too.

- How can you stand out? What do you know about – more than most people? Really – truthfully? Your job? A piece of software? Politics? Music? Clothes? Films? Clubs? Food? Childcare? Sport? Travel? Technology? Social networking? What?

Steve works in a restaurant and wants a day off at short notice. He makes sure he walks out of the door with his boss at the end of the evening – to neutral territory. He takes a few brief (and, of course, pre-planned) phone calls that sound important and make him look busy. He tells his boss he's helping someone by giving them advice about setting up a restaurant. He mentions he's had some good tips today – and says it's because he's been learning the menu inside out and talking to the customers about the way each dish has been cooked. He asks for the day off. By now it's hard to say no. And he gets what he wants.

How many celebrity techniques can you see in what Steve did to get what he wanted?

For meetings that you haven't planned, or are not necessarily formal ones around a big table, here's what you do. You never allow anyone to catch you unawares. That would be them striking first, and you want to strike first (see pages 106–107) – not them. You say you're a bit tied up, in a rush, on your way to another meeting, all the time breaking your non-verbal connection (see pages 85–88) with them (for example, turning slightly away, looking at your watch, putting one foot out as if you're about to stride off). Ask them to call you later to fix a time. You don't call them. You tell them to call you. If you can. If that would seem rude, then call them after a short delay. Keep them waiting for a bit. Now you've got a chance to think in advance about what you want from the conversation and which aspects of your celebrity you can use. You're back in charge.

If we're talking about one of those meetings with your boss – and your boss only – in your boss's office, in all honesty you're probably not going to be able to move it to your territory. If you can – go for it. If you can't, don't worry. As you walk into the office, turn round and close the door behind you. Do not ask if it's OK. Just do it. Claim some territory in there. Make sure you do it before they ask you to. Take a seat before you're invited. And if you're sitting across the desk, claim some of that desk space for your stuff. If you're both sitting in an informal area – say where there's a sofa or chairs or something – try to go for the highest area.

Never go into the corner. No one likes being backed into a corner. You want to be slightly looking down at him or her if you can. If not, sit back, cross your legs, look comfortable. Go for the chair over the sofa if you can. If you have no choice but the sofa, then perhaps your back is sore that day. If, on the other hand, your back is notoriously sturdy, take ownership of the sofa with your body. Think of it as your own sofa at home. It's your territory. Stretch one arm out along the back of it and cross your legs. Comfy?

Don't take too many notes. If you really need to remember something, write it down by all means. But don't write stuff down for the sake of it. It will make you look subservient and willing. Yes, Sir, no, Sir. Celebrities don't look good taking notes. If they do need to write something down, they tend to use a nice notebook rather than a scruffy old pad from the stationery cupboard. And, separately, if you're busy writing stuff down, you're not paying attention. You're looking at the notebook, and your handwriting, rather than looking at their face and their non-verbal signals so that you can get a handle on what they're really thinking. Celebrities read rather than write.

One trick to watch out for when dealing with your boss – never ever answer the question 'What motivates you?' Well, not truthfully, anyway. Telling your boss what motivates you, what makes you tick, what gets you out of bed in the morning, is like handing him a loaded gun with the safety catch off. If he knows what you want, he has the power to give it to you, deny you it, or worse – give it to you and then take it away. Do not tell him. Lie to him and pretend it's something that, in truth, doesn't motivate you at all. Or dodge the question. Of course, there may be people other than your boss who will try this tactic. Now you know what to look out for.

## Away from work

Away from work, getting what you want works the same way – almost. Imagine you want someone new in your life – for the next five minutes or the next 50 years. It doesn't matter. Where are you most likely to meet that person? Probably on neutral territory. A lot of people meet each other at work or through mutual friends or in a bar or club. All neutral territory – just apply the same rules slightly differently.

Mandy likes going out on a Saturday night with her mates. They go to the nightclub in town, where there are lots of fit blokes. Here's how Mandy makes sure she stands out from the crowd. She makes sure she's with a crowd of friends, not just one or two. She dresses one notch 'up' from them. Only one notch, though, no more. She makes sure her group arrives slightly late, once the club is already pretty full. She makes sure she's at the front when they arrive. Just before she walks into the main dance-floor area, she pauses at the door for a few seconds and surveys the scene. Once she's led her group of friends through the doorway, she leads them to a prominent place where everyone can see them. When possible she books a seating area in advance, which is marked by a red rope. It doesn't cost them any money as long as they buy a certain amount from the bar all evening.

If the roped-off areas are full, she looks for high ground. Up the stairs, on a platform, by the stage – somewhere prominent. Once her group is settled, Mandy makes a huge event out of asking each of her friends individually what they would like to drink. They'll buy their rounds later but Mandy makes sure she is first. When Mandy goes to the bar (if she needs to – usually only if the roped-off areas are full), she gets chatting with the barman and, if she can, gets him to bring the drinks over. One more thing – from the moment Mandy arrived, she had her eye open for anyone she even vaguely recognized. And when she saw them, she waved, said hello loudly, and made sure as many people as possible saw it. You can't have failed to notice, Mandy has arrived. Mandy wants the fit blokes to notice her, in a good way. And it's hard not to.

If there's someone you like at work and you want to make an impression on them, be like Sharon in her office. Don't be available straight away. If everyone's going out for a drink after work, be busy on the first occasion or two. Or say you've got something to do first, and turn up late. Or leave early. Create a sense of mystique. Make them feel fortunate when you are there for them. If someone's trying to set you up with someone, make it slightly – I said slightly – difficult. Be difficult to pin down. Look busy. Make them work a little harder to get hold of you than they expect.

If you're out and about and you see someone you like, the same applies. Never go up to them and talk to them first. Remember the rule about territories (see pages 128–129). Ideally, you want them to come to your territory. How do you do that? Connect with them. Get connection from afar, from across the room, unconsciously and non-verbally. They'll make the first move most of the time, if they're interested – even if it's just a smile or a longer look. Once that happens, you're in charge. Wait and they will come to you. Most of the time. If they don't – and eventually you bow to temptation and go over to them, you still need to make yourself seem slightly unavailable.

If possible, talk first to a friend of that person – and make your non-verbal signals (see pages 85–88) appear very slightly stand-offish to the person you're interested in. Turn your body slightly away from them while you're talking to their friend – but not completely. Be ambiguous. You want the person you're interested in to be trying to get your attention and to feel slightly excluded at first. You want them to start working to become involved in your conversation. You want them to feel your celebrity before they can talk to you.

If appropriate, you need to come across as busy too. Break off from the conversation and make a phone call. Be longer than they expect. Or go and talk to other people for a bit – again, for longer than they expect. Not too long so they give up on you – there's a fine line to tread. And you'll know where that line is because you can now read their non-verbal signals.

Just like in the office, you need to set the agenda. If you're going to suggest a drink, don't just do that – suggest the kind of drink you both should have. Suggest where you sit, where you stand, where you eat. If you're going to move on, suggest when you do it and where you go. Before long, you'll have created a basic autopilot (see pages 41–46) in their mind that you set the agenda, you're in charge and you make the decisions. Just like in the office.

If you happen to be with someone who likes to set the agenda themselves, then you need to claim some of it back. Knowledge and expertise is how you do it. Choose something to be an authority on. For example, if this person suggests eating at a certain restaurant or going to a particular bar, say something like 'Oh – I was there a week ago and it wasn't that good, because . . .' Trump their expertise – even if it's only because you're suggesting you've done something more recently than them. Dismiss what they have said with one hand. A subtle flick of the wrist will do it. Their unconscious will pick it up. Do it with books, films, TV shows, the theatre, music, you name it.

If there are times when you don't have a specific objective in mind, that's fine – just go with the flow. If you've fixed your mind on something that you really want, going with the flow will rarely get you it. Most people are predictable and don't have fully formed objectives in mind most of the time. That makes your life easier when there's something you want.

I need to talk to you about your dress. Or your trousers. The next time someone says to you that it's what's on the inside that counts, ask yourself why they feel the need to say that. Are they giving themselves permission to look a mess? Why would you – or anyone else – take the time to find out what's on the inside of somebody, if the way they look just doesn't give you any incentive to do that?

Your brain is greater than any of us. It's evolved over millions of years. If it decides, within a split second of meeting someone new, that they're not worth knowing because of the way they look, then everything else becomes unnecessarily difficult. Given the time and the inclination, people can, of course, overcome the brain's instinctive and immediate reactions. But why make life complicated? Give other people's brains a chance to react positively to you straight away by looking good. Looking good is a big part of looking the part. The part of a celebrity.

Looking good means looking as good as you possibly can. Whatever your budget, your taste, your look, your shape or your size. Make the most of yourself, and remember you want to be a notch 'up' from the people you want to influence to get what you want. Looking good means you have to feel good. Whatever's going on inside is obvious on the outside – however much you try to pretend. You've probably heard people say 'You are what you wear.' I don't agree. But you do feel what you wear.

---

### DO THIS

- Put on a suit or something very smart. How do you feel? Imagine sitting and watching your favourite TV show in that outfit. In fact, don't just imagine it, do it if you can!

- Put on an old T-shirt and old jogging bottoms. How do you feel? Imagine being interviewed for a job on the phone (so no one can see you) in those clothes. Would you feel right?

- Put on smart casual clothes – including a really smart pair of shoes. How do you feel? Imagine popping out to the shops quickly and getting some milk. Do that, too, if you have time.

Did each outfit make you feel different? And did each suggested activity seem a bit odd for each outfit? That's because the clothes you wear – and what you associate them with – fire off your autopilots. If you put on a suit or something formal, your brain goes into formal mode.

If you put casual clothing on – or the sort of comfortable clothes that you relax in at home, your brain goes into a 'relaxing' autopilot and would actually find it hard to be 'formal'. Wearing smart casual clothes to do something as mundane as pop out for some milk feels odd – right? Your clothes control the chemistry in your brain because of the associations that you've built up over the years. That chemistry, in turn, controls the way you behave and come across. Clothes are crucial.

What you wear has as much effect on your own brain as on other people's. Looking good and wearing the right clothes for the right occasion has a direct impact on your physiology – whether you try to fight it or not. And you know how your physiology affects your brain because I mentioned it earlier. What do celebrities hate most? Being caught by paparazzi in their jogging pants with messy hair and looking like they've just got out of bed. Why? Because it affects their celebrity and makes them normal like everyone else. And vulnerable. And not in control. And that doesn't help them get what they want.

If you're chatting to someone and you want to use your celebrity to get what you want, then – once again – leaning forward, smiling and nodding a lot is not the way to do it. You can do that if you just need to get connection but not if you're using your celebrity. Crossing your arms and your legs will help here, and so will looking away from time to time. Keep your head still, like in those meetings. The person needs to feel fortunate to be in your company. Sit back, literally, and get what you want. If you're going to leave early (as you should), let people know in advance. They'll see your time as precious.

Frowning from time to time is effective outside of work, too. Look confused at times and tell people you're not sure what they mean. Make them repeat themselves. Get them to work hard in your company. But not for too long at a time. Just when they're least expecting it, lean in – smile and be genuinely warm. Before you pull back again. You'll confuse them a bit but that's good, as you know.

The thing about your brain is that it's really clever. It's really sophisticated. Your gut instinct is usually right because your brain has processed lots of crucial pictures, sounds and feelings in a split second. That's why you should usually go with your gut. The trouble with what I've just said is that I've said it before. And you probably knew what I was going to say next. Which means you were not confused in any way – and that freed up your own mind to drift. You may have allowed your internal dialogue to start going on about something else, or some irrelevant pictures to creep in. You may have started thinking about what you are going to eat later. Or the colour of that wall over there. Whatever it was, you distanced yourself from me briefly. You see, a little bit of confusion leads to learning. And it keeps your attention.

Helen got her ex-boyfriend interested again. She met him at her favourite coffee shop that she and her friends always go to. She looked great that day – and she felt great in her new clothes. Quite a few of the other people in the coffee shop said hello to her as she walked in. Of course they did, they were friends and she'd asked them to in advance. But he didn't know that. Helen got most of the attention in there. She looked popular. It was at this point that he started having a rethink and wondered if splitting up with her had been the right move after all. While they were there, her phone went a couple of times but she didn't answer it. She told him she would call them back later. She told him she'd be up for going out one Saturday night but it would have to be when she got back from a big work conference next week. It was hard to say no to that.

---

**DO THIS**

Do this the next time you need to get off a bus or a train, or out of a lift or a busy shop, and there's a crowd of people waiting to get on the bus or train or come into the lift or the shop. Maybe it's rush hour or maybe it's just a busy shopping day.

Before you walk forward, just pause and stand at the doorway for slightly longer than they would expect you to. It's usually a second or two but it feels like longer. Watch the crowd part in front of you, allowing you to move forward unimpeded. Congratulations, you've just used your celebrity.

I've got a weak bladder. I think I told you earlier. I need to use the boys' room a lot. And whenever I'm caught short and I need to go, there seems to be nowhere available. So I use my celebrity. I walk into any bar, pub or coffee shop, chatting away to nobody on my mobile. I walk straight to the Gents, without looking at anyone, because I'm concentrating on my imaginary phone call. It's almost impossible to stop me. I'm always dressed quite well but not well enough to get away with this in a really posh restaurant. So I don't choose really posh restaurants. If any staff challenged me – and they never have – I would just keep walking, hold up my hand, point to my phone and ask them to give me two minutes as I carried on towards the Gents. Would you say no to that?

To get a real idea of how powerful it can be when people use their celebrity, think about when you've been on the receiving end. Imagine you're standing in a hotel reception area and a casually dressed man (possibly wearing flip flops and a shell necklace) comes up to you and asks you nicely if he can help you with your bags. What would you do?

### Remember This
*Celebrity is not who you are, it's what you do. We all can use our celebrity.*

What about if he was a smartly dressed man?

And what about if he was a man in a suit and wearing a name badge? You'd assume he worked for the hotel and let him carry your bags, wouldn't you?

What about if a man in a high-visibility jacket and a hard hat walked into your house, through the front door, said he was doing some building work next door and apologized for the noise of the drilling in advance? This happened to a friend who was a bit surprised to see him at first, but then thanked him for letting her know, saw him out and then went upstairs to do something. The drilling outside began, as expected. It wasn't as loud as she thought it would be. While she was upstairs, the man in the hard hat and the high-visibility jacket came back in and helped himself to everything in her handbags. Then he let himself back out, collected his mate (who was doing the drilling) and waved goodbye to her through the upstairs window as he left. She waved back.

Let's do an autopilot check at this point – initial surprise that a stranger has walked into the house; usually a cause for alarm. But overridden in an instant by the autopilot that says 'man in high-vis jacket and hard hat has some authority/expertise, has a job to do, and may well have a good reason for walking into your house'. The fact that he walked into her house without asking fired off the 'It must be OK – a part of his job – otherwise no person would do that' autopilot. In other words, it was hard to say no. And finally, the drilling began as he said it would – firing off the autopilot which said 'He said I'd hear drilling – and I'm hearing drilling. So everything he says is true, in that case.' Add to that the fact that the drilling noise was consistent with what she thought his job was and what his uniform told her his job was. Powerful stuff, you see. In the wrong hands, as well as the right ones.

You're sitting in a restaurant and a very smartly dressed man (no uniform, just smartly dressed) walks up to your table and asks you if you're enjoying your meal. What do you say? And what do you assume? Who have your autopilots told you he is? Your autopilots will assume that someone is in authority, or in charge, if they say the right things, behave in the right way, wear the right clothes and use the right props. If they do all that, your autopilots will promote them to celebrity status straight away, without you even questioning it consciously. So, do you want to have that effect on other people's autopilots to get what you want? It goes without saying that I'm talking about legal stuff, not illegal stuff.

A particularly cunning estate agent – we'll call him Will – wanted to sell me what is now my home. This was before I knew any of the stuff that I've told you about in this book. Notice how many times someone made it hard for me to say no.

He showed me round the flat. It's a nice flat. One balcony and a roof terrace. It was easily the nicest flat that he'd shown me – and he'd shown me about five in the area. I told him I liked it. *Mistake number one.* I told him I was thinking about putting in an offer. *Mistake number two.* He told me the current owners had suffered a disappointing last-minute withdrawal from someone they thought was in the bag. *Tactic number one.* He said that, for that reason, they wouldn't accept an offer lower than the asking price because they felt they'd been treated badly enough already and were taking no nonsense. *Tactic number two*. I said OK. *Mistake number three*. I didn't want to give them the asking price so I made a lower offer anyway – but the offer was higher than I would have made had he not said all this. *Mistake number four*. He said, 'Hmmm. I'm not sure they'll be up for it. Why don't I arrange for you to meet them? If they like you, they might say yes.' *Tactic number three*. I said, 'Good idea, OK.' *Mistake number five*.

Why do people suspend their belief and imagine – even though they know it's not true – that the estate agent is working on behalf of the buyer? What an autopilot. Well, that was my autopilot at least. Your rulebook might be different. How do they do that? *Tactic number four*. *Mistake number six*.

I arrived at the flat to meet Mark and his wife. Mark invited me in and we all sat down in the kitchen (*tactic number five, mistake number seven*) to chat and get to know each other. Why? No idea. He offered me a beer. We all had a beer and he talked about how he, his wife and his friends often sat in this kitchen with the balcony doors open drinking beer with their friends at weekends. *Tactic number six*. He asked me if there was anything I wanted to buy from him, that he could leave for me. *Tactic number seven*. I said, 'Actually, there may well be.' *Mistake number eight*. He suggested the washing machine, the dishwasher, and asked if I wanted any furniture. I replied that I needed a new sofa. He told me the price he wanted. It was quite reasonable. I agreed.

*Mistake number nine*. It was time for me to go, so I got up. Mark's wife gave me their contact details and said they weren't moving very far away and would love to come round and 'see what you've done with the place, once you've moved in'. *Tactic number eight.* I agreed verbally but thought privately 'Are you mad? I don't even know you.' *Smart move number one* (and the only one!).

As soon as I got home, I rang Will and said I loved the flat and would definitely like to proceed. Would Mark and his wife accept my offer now that I'd met them? I imagined they would, as we'd even agreed a separate, private transaction on the washing machine, dishwasher and sofa. Will sounded delighted and said he would ring Mark straight away and call me straight back. *Tactic number nine.* Will didn't call back. *Tactic number 10.* A day later, I was so on tenterhooks that I rang him. *Mistake number 10.* Will sounded deflated. *Tactic number 11.* 'Mark and his wife were really pleased to meet you but, on reflection, they really can't come down from their asking price, especially as you've got a pretty good deal on the washing machine, dishwasher and sofa.' *Tactic number 12.* As I write this story, I really can't quite believe it, still – all these years later. Some people's rulebooks! Does yours say, 'Walk this way, walk all over me and walk away with all my money?' Mine did.

I raised my offer to the asking price. *Mistake number 11.* Mark accepted. I moved in. It's a second-floor flat with no lift. Straight away I discovered that the staircase is too narrow to accommodate large pieces of furniture. Or even medium-sized, for that matter. I spent a long time shopping around for small items. I also spent a lot of time in IKEA buying flatpack.

Will wanted to get maximum commission from the sale of Mark's flat. He was probably going on an expensive diving holiday in the Seychelles the following month. He got what he wanted.

Mark and his wife wanted to sell their flat at a top-end price without having to pay high fees to a specialist removal company. You know the ones – the ones who have to take your windows out to extract large washing machines, dishwashers and L-shaped sofas using a crane. Mark also wanted to avoid the cost of the expensive, temporary parking permit for the crane. He also wanted more cash – on top of the asking price. Mark got what he wanted.

I never really liked the sofa. I'm not sure why I agreed to buy it in the first place. I put up with it for a couple of years until I could bear it no more. But how was I going to get rid of it without putting my flat up for sale? A mate of mine ended up coming round with a saw and he chopped it up into tiny pieces so that I could dispose of it in bin bags. Seeing what my mate did to that sofa, I was sorely tempted to send him round to Mark and his wife's new house (I had their address and phone number, remember). But all Mark and his wife had done was get what they want. Via a different rulebook, admittedly, but that's fine now that I know about people's rulebooks. Instead of sending my friend to their house with his saw, I decided to learn from Mark and his wife. And Will.

What did I learn about the power of celebrity? Will is an estate agent, an expert, a specialist. He was busy, he was aloof, he was one step ahead. I was never certain of getting hold of him and I felt fortunate when I did. Whatever he said, I listened to. He told me they wouldn't accept any offers, then he told me they might if they met me, but then he told me they wouldn't after all. I listened and believed him each time. Will, Mark and his wife then got me into the flat. Mark's territory. And his wife's. Who asked me in? Who asked me to sit down? Who offered me a beer? Who wanted to seal the deal on his washing machine, dishwasher and sofa while I was on his territory? Who's in charge here?

Who's in charge when you have visitors at your home? (That's why Ann Summers lingerie parties work so well in people's homes.) Who said he would call me straight back, once I'd been to see Mark and his wife. Who didn't call me straight back? Who ended up calling? Who was in charge all the way? Who were the celebrities?

I got what I wanted, too. True. I got the flat and I'm glad I did. I love it. But I had to pay. More than I should have. Well done, Mark. You got what you wanted. And Will.

---

**ALERT!** *How to achieve exactly the opposite of what this book is intended to achieve –*

If you have people over, this doesn't mean you can behave like a total moron just because it's your house. Remember, everything Will and Mark did was generous and welcoming, at least on the surface.

---

You don't have to be an estate agent or a warrant officer in the army (see pages 110–111) to use your celebrity, as you now know. Using your celebrity is like carrying a loaded gun, so use it wisely. If you happened to be maniacal, deranged, obsessive, unhinged and a thoroughly bad person, then you'd probably start a cult and use these techniques to relieve innocent and vulnerable people of all their money, their liberty and freedom of thought before getting them all to top themselves at the same time. This stuff is powerful. Use it properly and well – and keep your peripheral eyes peeled for the scumbags who don't.

You should use your celebrity if you haven't succeeded – or know you won't succeed – in just getting connection (see chapter 9). The human brain is programmed to bow to authority and submit to the leader of the pack. Using your celebrity is the best option if getting what you want is the most important thing to you and you're not too bothered what people think.

Celebrity is not about being famous, but breaking celebrity behaviour down to its component parts and then copying it to an everyday context. It is about being on your territory, being in demand, looking the part and standing out from the crowd. This will make you come across as in charge, in authority, special, an expert, individual, in demand, busy, popular, one step ahead, or ever so slightly unapproachable.

When you want to use your celebrity, it helps to imagine you *are* your favourite celebrity. Don't just pretend, you know how to do it properly with your internal dialogue and pictures. Like Meryl.

# 13

# Persuasion Technique Number 4: Human or Inhuman

You are a human. I am a human. I am trying to be human with you. It's difficult because you only know me from what I'm writing. You're not just human, though. You can be inhuman when you want. You have the choice. Always. Sometimes you'll get what you want by being human. Other times you'll get it by being inhuman. Let me explain.

Being human means being you. Being personally you. The person you are when you're with your family, your friends and the people that know you well. What's your first name? Imagine writing your name here _ _ _ _ _ _ _ _ _

That's you being human.

So how can you be inhuman? Easy. You put up a barrier so you can hide behind it. You can hide behind your job, your title, your email, a text message, someone else's orders, an organization, a club, a website, you name it. Being inhuman helps if you need to do something that humans find difficult. If you fire someone, you're actually depriving them of their job and their livelihood. That's hard, when you think about it. But if you do it in the name of the company, it's much easier. If you want to cancel a night out with someone at the last minute, calling them and explaining yourself is harder than cancelling by text and saying you'll call them tomorrow. Saying no to someone is easier if you've got something to hide behind.

You can choose to be human or inhuman whenever you want. If one doesn't work, flip to the other. You're adaptable.

Stop. Just before you press the red button, there is a package for you. You remember that red button. If you went for the hired assassin option in the chapter about Rulebooks (see page 57), just before you make that call – stop. Sometimes, even if you're set on something, something might happen that means you've got to change course (adapt!) at the last minute.

There's a brown envelope somewhere in the picture that you have in your mind right now. Packages are often in brown envelopes. This one is tied up with string. Your name is on it in block capital letters. I have a feeling your package has a one or a six on it.

Take the parcel and unpack it. Put the DVD in your DVD player and press play.

'Please, please. I'm begging you. Please don't. I'm Rob. I have two children. Think of my family. Think of my kids. What are they going to do without me? They need their dad. Who's going to look after them? Who's going to feed them? Who's going to protect them? Please. You were a kid once. Who took care of you? It's OK, Jess, it's OK.

Daddy's here. Daddy'll look after you and Tom. Daddy'll keep you safe.'

Now you've met Rob, isn't it harder to say no to him? I'm imagining that your finger is further away from that red button than it was a few moments ago. Do you really want to make that call?

It is much more difficult to press that button now because your victims are more real, more human. You saw their faces, you heard their voices and you know their names. If staying alive is what Rob wants for him and his kids, being human is more likely to help him.

Here's an example of what people can do when they're being inhuman. There's a man in a black hooded top with a white mask. He's really angry. The crowd is angry. He's not getting what he wants.

He wants an end to world poverty, capitalism and global warming. He's trying to get what he wants in the only way that he knows how. Angrily. Before he can do anything, a massive wall of black pushes him to the ground. He's winded. He sees red. He lashes out with a piece of wood at the wall of black. And hits a human.

Samantha Jones looks down at David's battered face. Joel, who's five, wants his daddy to play in the garden like they always do on Sundays. David can't play in the garden today. He won't be playing for a while. He'll still be in hospital for his 26th birthday on Wednesday. His mum, Jan, had never wanted him to join the police.

How would the man in the black hooded top have reacted if

he'd seen David Jones, husband of Samantha, father of Joel and son of Jan in front of him, rather than one of a row of identical policemen forming a wall of black?

An email was sent to me the other day. It said:

Dear Mark

I am not a sensitive person by nature, but I have to say that I am feeling a little hurt. We've invited you into our Club, but you've clearly decided not to join.

So, as a one-off attempt at sheer bribery, I'm offering you your first, trial Club case HALF PRICE at just £47.88 (that's a ridiculously low £3.99 a bottle!). Plus, two FREE gifts, worth £30. That's an overall saving of nearly £80.

That email held my attention. It was sent to *me* so I said yes! It was far better than the usual ones that normally go like this:

SPECIAL SUMMER OFFER
Cases of wine now half price. Please fill in this form
to be eligible for your discount.

What pictures pop into your head when I mention these brands?

Apple
Nike
Coca-Cola
Persil

Ford

BBC

Nescafé

Snickers

And with this one – *who* pops into your head?

Virgin.

Richard Branson, right? A human, rather than an object or a thing. Don't get me wrong. They're all good brands. But which one is going to find it easiest to sell a *range* of products? Which one is most likely to be successful *whatever* it produces? Being human can get you what you want, too.

Here's an example of someone who wasn't getting what he wanted by being inhuman. Without knowing (because he hadn't read this book) he suddenly got what he wanted when he became human.

Knightrider1 was online a lot. Sarah spent a fair amount of time chatting on the dating site, match.com. She was 36 and felt like time was running out. She'd been out on a few dates but nothing serious ever came of them. She'd chatted to Knightrider1 quite a few times. He always said hello to her when he saw her online. She replied politely but, from his picture, she knew he wasn't her type. Knightrider1 looked nothing like 'The Hoff'. Knightrider1 really liked Sarah's picture. It's a strange world. There they were tapping away at each other, him into her but her not keen on him, and neither of them realized they lived half a mile apart.

The Duke of York is a pub. Sarah goes there quite a lot. She's had a few hot dates in there but they cooled down quickly. Before the end of each date, more often than not, Sarah had more than once looked longingly at the windows in the Ladies and wished the bars hadn't been there. Maybe they were put there by match.com. Or the same people who supplied the condom machine next to the basin by the door.

Sarah was with Monica who she used to work with. Monica had just got divorced. They were tucking into a bottle of New Zealand Sauvignon Blanc and were sharing a plate of nachos and a retro sandwich (fishfingers in lime mayonnaise on white crusty bread). Sarah was about one eighth of the way through a slightly bigger than advisable mouthful of rectangular cod when she felt a tap on her shoulder.

'Sarah!'

Sarah was speechless. Partly because somehow Knightrider1 had come alive and was standing above her in her local pub, where she went for bottles of Sauvignon Blanc with Monica, and partly because her mouth was stuffed full of what had once been a perfectly innocent cod, swimming around with his cod mates at the bottom of the sea. Gills, fins, tail, scales. The lot. If you want to make a fish look unlike a fish so that kids eat it, then you make it into a finger of fish. Sorry – that was a tiny tangent.

'I'm Michael, from match.com, can I get you a drink?'

The word 'no' didn't cross Sarah's mind. Michael spoke with a cheeky Irish charm. He was much taller than she had imagined. When he smiled, he had a cute dimple. And really, really broad shoulders! If only Michael had known about being 'human or inhuman', he'd have got together with Sarah a lot sooner. Sarah and Michael are looking forward to the birth of their baby in September.

Have you ever watched *Comic Relief*? The programme is really moving. It tells you stories about malaria, famine, children in desperate circumstances around the world, some in the UK, moving pictures of people in dire need. You see their faces, know their names and hear their voices. The programme reminds you that this woman could be your mother, this child could be your son and this girl could be your granddaughter. It is difficult to say no to that. Even a few of the show's presenters have been known to shed the odd tear. I admit it, I get a lump in my throat. (To show how effective this is, in 2009 *Comic Relief* raised £78 million.)

People like humans.

But they don't like traffic wardens, estate agents, journalists (especially newspaper ones), bankers, or tax collectors – so traffic wardens, estate agents, journalists, bankers and tax collectors make sure they're as inhuman as possible.

This never happens:

'Hi, I'm Jenny, and I'm your traffic warden for the day. My favourite colours are yellow and black, I'm a Virgo and my favourite food is Italian. I'm delighted to present you with this parking ticket for £60. What's your name, and how are you? Nice car, by the way. Have you had it long?'

or

'Hey mate,' (holds out hand) 'I'm Will. Before you decide on what price you want to put your house up for, can I just let you know that I earn all my money from you. So the more you spend, the happier I am. My girlfriend, Tara, is even happier. We're going to the Seychelles next month and I'm saving up to buy us brand-new diving suits. I've just done my PADI.'

or

'Hello, my name is Vicky. I just thought I'd let you know that I'm going to go through your dustbins and dig out some dirt about you so I can write an article and get my pay rise next month. Don't worry. I won't take any notice of any other personal stuff that I don't need for the story – like any evidence that Nick stayed over last night and that used tube of ointment.

or

'Peter, I'm so pleased you've asked to borrow this money. You and Claire are such a nice couple and you really deserve that holiday. I know you've been working hard all year and it's not been easy, especially since Claire's mother's hip operation. Deirdre sends her love.'

or

'Hello, Sandra speaking, your personal tax manager. Is that you, John? Thanks for dropping me a line to let me know that you can't pay your income tax this year. I'm sure your mate, Cliff, meant well with that 100–1 tip. Better luck next time. I am going to need the payment, though, by a week on Tuesday. Can you give me a shout? You've got my direct line. I'm in between 9 a.m. and 6 p.m. but I'm not in on Thursday because I'm taking my cat to the vet.'

Sometimes getting what you want means being human. And sometimes getting what you want means being inhuman. Being inhuman works a bit like this:

Uniform, name of organization you're acting for, badge, number, no first names, no hello, no reply, rank or status, client/supplier, employer/employee, 'as your manager, I . . .', 'this is a business decision', 'it's for the good of everyone', blaming inhuman elements that you can't control – like the traffic, everything about being in the military, an ID pass, reminding people of your statutory rights as a customer, staying in your office rather than mixing with the staff, Doctor, Professor, Constable, Officer, Sir, Prime Minister, Your Majesty, President, Group Chief Executive and Managing Director, Your Honour, Ma'am, Coach, Mr, Mrs, Miss, National Sales Director – Trading, National Sales Director – Operations, 'the public', 'the Chinese', 'the French', 'Africa', 'the Western world', 'the rich', 'the poor', 'The Daily Telegraph', 'the BBC has learned', 'the BBC understands that . . .', 'I need to stay late for this meeting, darling, I'm a Director and that's what the company expects from me.' And of course there are the things I mentioned much earlier, like email, Facebook, texting, MSN, blogging, chat forums, Twitter, MySpace – even the faceless telephone when you think about it.

It's hard to be human, these days, isn't it?

---

**DO THIS**

1. Think of a recent time when you came up against someone and found it difficult to get what you wanted.

2. Was that person being human or inhuman?

3. Were you being human or inhuman?

4. What difference would it have made if you'd been the opposite of what you answered in step 3?

---

I was redecorating my house a few years ago. I'm rubbish at DIY and I bought way too much plaster. When I'd finished the work, I decided to take what I had left back to the DIY shop where I'd bought it and get a refund.

I wheeled a massive trolley stacked full of plaster into the shop and said, 'Hello, I'd like to return this, please.'

The guy behind the counter said, 'Sorry, plaster is a non-returnable item.'

I showed him the receipt and I told him I hadn't opened the bags but it seemed to go over his head. All he kept saying was

'Sorry, plaster is a non-returnable item.' By this time, it had turned into a full-blown argument – the sort of argument that makes everyone stop what they're doing and watch but pretend they're not. Oh come on, we've all done it.

I was livid. I told him this was not the level of customer service I would expect from a big store like this one and I reminded him of my statutory rights as a consumer (obviously I knew next to nothing about my statutory rights, like most people, but, like most people, I thought I'd give it a go anyway).

He answered by listing my statutory rights back to me. But way more accurately. Git. I did not get what I wanted because I'd made it so easy for him to say no. If I'd known about being human and inhuman, I'd have probably changed tack at this point. I'd have probably told him I'd come a long way to bring the plaster back, my pregnant wife was in the car with my three-year-old son (true), that I used this store a lot and I was usually served by Valerie who helped me out every time I came in.

I got a call from a radio station the other day. They wanted to talk to me about child psychology – and what makes some kids commit violent acts. It was difficult for me to say no as soon as I answered the phone. The radio station – just by the fact that it's a radio station – uses its celebrity to get people to

> **Remember This**
>
> *As an adaptable person, the most important thing to remember is that you always have the choice of switching between being human and inhuman. There is no set formula for either but there is a rule of thumb: doing the opposite of what the person is doing will often get you what you want.*

appear on it. Small tangent, I know. This chapter is about being human and inhuman.

The interviewer had the sort of voice that wore a large medallion and had Hollywood-white teeth. It reminded me a bit of my mum and dad's wallpaper. Anyway, there was a story in the news about two kids who had hurt another couple of kids so badly that they nearly died. He wanted to know what drives such young people to do such hideous things to other kids and – more importantly – whether this happened more today than in the past.

I told him this. For a change, I used a bit of jargon. I said aggressive behaviour can be learned but is not necessarily *used*; it tends to be *used* only when a reward is available or it leads to some kind of other gain; aggressive behaviours are learned through reinforcement and imitation of aggressive examples; the more people get reports of violence, the more 'proof' their unconscious has that violence is in some way acceptable and they believe that aggression becomes in some way a legitimate way of achieving a goal.

I told him TV and video games disinhibit people. Through their realistic imitation of violence they can create a dehuman-ized attitude towards violence in some people. Too many violent video games, films or factual programmes – particularly if you're a kid – can make violent acts against other people seem more OK than they are. And that's not OK.

Without the jargon, being inhuman makes it possible to do all kinds of things that humans wouldn't normally do.

My nephew's got a Wii. You know what Wii means. Yes. He has a game that gets you to imitate strangling and stabbing someone to win. If you've played with a Wii before, you'll know that this isn't just pressing buttons. You actually have to stand in front of your TV and physically go through the motions of strangling and stabbing, holding a Wii controller (with nunchuck attachment) in your hands. I wonder what will happen when true virtual reality arrives?

People around you are humanizing and dehumanizing all the time to get what they want. The difference is – they don't know they're doing it. Someone, somewhere – probably in authority – has told them to do it like that because it works. But they didn't know why, either. They still don't. Unlike you, people are not consciously aware of how they do it, why they do it and how much it can get them. Unlike you. Now.

People who humanize to get what they want do it like this:

'Hi, hon. I know you're my boss and everything but I saw this ring when I was on holiday and I knew you'd love it.' She got what she wanted.

I got a letter the other day from a leading media company. It said, 'Hi Scott. I just thought I'd let you know you can now get our broadband cable TV in Acacia Avenue (my address!).' They got what they wanted.

I once worked with a bloke who was always petrified of being made redundant. He was right to be, because his job wasn't all that necessary and was often up for discussion around the board table. He made a point of covering his desk with photographs of his wife and children. Every morning, he would give you a blow-by-blow account of everything that he and his family had done the night before, what his kids were up to and how they were getting on at school. They didn't make him redundant but the business really should have done. He got what he wanted.

'I don't fancy Chinese tonight. Can't we have Thai? The man who runs the restaurant is really nice and friendly. He always remembers my name and asks me how the kids are.' Two people got what they wanted there.

'Come on, Jack, eat it all up. Do it for Mummy. There's a good boy. Do it for me now, go on, Jack. Good boy.' He did what she wanted. Well, sometimes.

'Hello, Peter Bates, chief executive. Pleased to meet you. You must be Simon Porter.'

'Hi, Peter. Yep – I'm Simon. Good to meet you.'

'So, Simon. Pull up a chair. Can I get you a coffee? Then we can talk through your CV.' Look how Simon made Peter Bates more human by being human himself. He got the job.

This one needs no explanation. Use it whenever you want.

'No, Tom, let's not go out. Tell you what, I'll cook you dinner, we'll have a bottle of wine and curl up on the sofa. Just you and me. You deserve a bit of pampering. You've worked really hard all week. You always find it difficult to relax, so let me help you, babe.' She knew his ex-girlfriend was going to be there and she really didn't want her to get what she wanted.

(Background music: 'You Raise Me Up')
   'Hi, I'm Shane's mum.'
   'Hello, I'm Shane's Gran and I'm sitting in his messy bedroom now. Look! He's had that toy guitar since he was three.'
   'Hello, Shane. Good luck to you from everyone in class 3E.'
   (The *X Factor* gets what it wants.)

'Hello. I'm Chris, the chairman.' (I'm not sure what he wanted.) 'Hi, sorry to bother you at home. I need to cancel our meeting in the morning because my nephew has been rushed to hospital with suspected appendicitis and I need to stay at home to look after his little brother while everyone's at the hospital.' (Try saying no to that, whatever it says in your rulebook – see chapter 4.)

People who need to be inhuman to get what they want do it like this:

'Smith, Jones. You're wanted in the headmaster's office immediately. Hurry up but do not run.'
   (Mr Dunning always got what he wanted.)

Or this:

'To all staff,

As you know, this company has finalized an agreement to merge with You Need This Ltd with effect from the beginning of next month. The newly formed company has taken the decision to shed a number of posts across the board to maximize this company's competitiveness in this challenging commercial environment.'

(Thirty people from the sales department, all of whom had been underperforming for years, lost their jobs.)

'Here's your cheque. There's the door.'

(Tracy – see pages 50–53 – got what she wanted. Until she ran out of drinking buddies.)

Or this:

'Dear Jim,

Thank you for your email. I note your request for flexible working hours to accommodate your longer journey to work now that you have changed address. I regret to inform you that company policy requires all employees, without exception, to arrive before 9.30 a.m. weekdays due to the nature of our business.'

(The boss won. Jim could have humanized to increase the chances of getting what he wanted. Company policy can be broken.)

Or this:

crazy day. stuk in trafic. wont make this eve. soz. c u 2mrw

A text message with a closing 'see you tomorrow' gets you out of any debate or peer pressure. If that's what you want.

Sometimes, people get it wrong. They're human when they should be inhuman. Or the other way round.

Politicians who kiss babies.

Royal families who initially don't fly a flag at half-mast above the palace because of 'protocol' despite an overwhel-mingly and uncharacteristically heart-on-sleeve reaction of grief across a normally very reserved population.

Teachers who introduce themselves by their first name.

Energy suppliers who employ telesales staff and instruct them to ask you 'How's your day been so far?' in a crude and contrived way to get connection with you. They need this book.

Managers who refer stressed employees to the Human Resources department instead of spending 10 minutes finding out what's stressing them out, over a cup of tea.

What's your favourite ad? Think about it now. Your favourite ad ever. I bet it's not a radio ad. Radio ads aren't as human because you can't see anyone. That's why TV ads are so much more expensive.

---

**DO THIS**

- Choose a person you want to influence.

- What could you do to be human?

- What could you do to be inhuman?

- Choose to start with either one, and do the other one if the first doesn't work.

---

## Conclusion

You can choose to be human or inhuman in any situation. Being human or inhuman can be used in conjunction with all the other techniques you'll read in this book.

Being human is being you, being personal – no barriers required. Being inhuman means you're hiding behind something – for example an organization, rules, another person, email or text.

As a rule of thumb, it works best to do the opposite of whatever the person you're trying to influence is doing.

Being inhuman is one of the rare times when it's sometimes better not to be face to face. Do this when you want to stop someone else getting what they want from you.

# 14

# Persuasion Technique Number 5: Give Them *Some* Credit

You know that using your celebrity is often the best way of getting what you want. Particularly if you've tried to get connection (see chapter 9) and it hasn't worked. Or if you just know that it won't work with that person. Using your celebrity – and being human or inhuman – are primarily about getting what you want. Whether they like you for it or not comes second.

If you need to get what you want *and* still have the person like you because you need to maintain a long-term relationship with them, then you're now in the right place.

You can probably think of someone who gets what they want, is no pushover and is popular too. It might be someone at work or it might be a friend. Now that you're thinking of that person, this is how he or she does it.

1. Give them some credit.

2. Give them *some* credit.

It only works if you say it out loud. Read number 1 out loud, somewhere private. Now read out number 2, but do it this way: stress the word 'some' more than any other word in the sentence. Give them *some* credit. What's the difference?

1. Give them some credit means: give them some credit. That's it. No real translation required. Take it at face value.

2. Give them *some* credit means: give them a bit of credit but not too much; not enough to make them think they're in charge.

As with using your celebrity, this technique is about showing people you're in control. Remember, you're the one getting what you want so you need to set the rules and guidelines. You're also the one in charge of dishing out credit – and how much. A bit like a bank manager. Think of it like that. Who's in charge in that relationship, even though you're the customer?

'Please, may I have a loan?'

'Yes, I will fill in your forms.'

'Yes, I will stay on hold and select option two.'

'Yes, I understand you might turn me down.'

'Yes, I'm still actually the paying customer and I'm going to be paying you a lot of interest for your services.'

It's amazing, isn't it, that the way you say some things has such an impact on someone's unconscious? More so, in many cases, than what you say. Think about how the meaning of sentences changes – depending on the emphasis – even if you use the same words.

**DO THIS**

How does the meaning of this sentence differ each time?

1. Give *them* some credit.

2. Give them *some* credit.

3. Give them some *credit.*

Now you've thought about that, I reckon you took each one to mean something like these:

1. Give credit to a certain group of people, rather than others.

2. (We've done this one).

3. Give those people credit rather than, say, criticizing them.

This chapter is about making people feel valued for their skills, experience or past achievements. Slightly. Remember, don't give them too much credit or they'll start to grab the balance of power from you.

Think of it like this: with one hand you're giving someone a controlled, limited level of credit in an area harmless to you. And with the other hand you are taking control of the situation so you can get what you want. Remember – you don't ever want to give credit for something you want to be in charge of.

For example: if I wanted to take an item of clothing back to the shop where I'd bought it, even though I'd worn it to a wedding. I wouldn't actually do this because my rulebook (see chapter 4) won't let me. But if it did, I might do it in this way.

I might give the sales assistant credit for being keen to offer good customer service. But I wouldn't give him or her any credit for their knowledge of clothes, fashion, how things look and fit or what goes with what.

I can hear your internal dialogue from here. It's saying 'OK, what do you mean? Give me some real examples!' OK. I'll use me. And me. We were both there.

I'll tell you what happened.
*And I'll point out the techniques being used.*

We had a meeting with a couple of people we'd been doing business with for a while. We got on well with them and found that we often agreed on things. It was all good. So good, that we thought we'd better get a second opinion, just to make sure what we wanted to talk about made good business sense. As you know, it's all very well getting on with people, but business is business and we didn't want to be blinded by the fact that we were all mates. So, we took a friend of ours, whose opinion we trusted, to the meeting to give us an objective view of what we were planning.

Let's talk about the numbers first: three of us and two of them. *Not ideal for them.* They decided quickly that what they wanted was to get this third person on board; as signed up to them and on the same page as we were. *They decided to give her some credit.*

They arrived at our office.
*Our territory. Not ideal for them either.*

We were our usual selves. We introduced them to Mel, our third person, and told them that she had come along to the meeting because of her experience in events. This was true – and the event we were planning had a big hospitality element. Our visitors, Harry and Sam, began to ask Mel enthusiastically about her past experience at organizing events.

Mel began to offer lots of information about herself, and – implicitly – how good she was at her job. They listened and threw in the odd question to keep her talking. The more she talked, the more she began to justify herself. The more she justified herself, the more they gave her *some* credit for what she could do. They showed her that they appreciated her experience in delivering hospitality and catering for big events for over 500 people, and acknowledged that this was not something they could do themselves.

*There are a few things going on here. Let's get inside Mel's head for a while. Firstly, on the surface, Mel is feeling valued. Her internal dialogue (see pages 19–23) is saying something like 'Brilliant, they care about what I've got to say. I'm needed here. I like it when I meet*

---

### Remember This

*Asking someone to explain all about what they're good at will usually result in them – eventually – justifying themselves as if they're in a job interview. If you wait long enough, that is. This fires off their 'job interview' autopilot (see pages 41–46) and they will feel unconsciously they're on the defensive.*

people who care about what I think and what I can do.' Mel's rulebook is backing up what her internal dialogue is saying by telling her that if people ask her questions, then they must be interested in her. This is happening because the questions are being asked nicely and with a smile.

Secondly, deep down in her unconscious, she is beginning to move on to the back foot. It's become very hard to say no. Having tried to take charge of this conversation at the beginning, she is now handing control to Harry and Sam by having to answer their questions. She begins by explaining her role and her job but – because they keep her talking for long enough – she moves automatically to justifying herself, as most people do. If you ever find yourself justifying yourself to anyone, you've immediately put them in charge.

Thirdly, the fact that they keep her talking about herself, and asking her to tell them more and more, tells her that they are listening to her with interest. We all like to be listened to. And everyone likes talking about themselves.

Fourthly, another reason why the conscious part of Mel's brain doesn't quite know what's really going on here is because it's busy making pictures, sounds and feelings about her, her job and why she's so good at it. It's easy to create pictures in other people's minds you want them to focus on, while you're busy getting what you want.

Fifthly, they have given her an area for her to specialize in: hospitality and catering at big events for over 500 people, based on her experience. Not hospitality in general! This is crucial. They have been very specific and selective about what they consider her speciality to be – and they have limited it to an area which they are happy to hand over to her fully.

When giving some credit, you give it to experience, past achievements and skills. You never refer to the person as an expert or as

*having expertise in an area. They might use those words themselves –*
*you don't. Experience, achievements and skills are one thing – expert-*
*ise and knowledge are power. You keep those for yourself. How would*
*you rather be regarded? As very skilled at or experienced in some-*
*thing – or an expert?*

It worked. They got what they wanted. Mel loved them, she
loved the idea and ended up working with us all on the project.
Mel did a great job in providing hospitality and catering at big
events for over 500 people. That's one thing I forgot to tell you.
The credit must be genuine, and it shouldn't matter much to
you. Choose something you really can give some credit for –
don't just make it up. You'll know what that is, probably
because you know how to get inside Grant's head already.
Remember him? He was the agent we mentioned earlier to tell
you how to read what's going on in someone's head and what
they want (see chapter 7).

If you can't work out what you can give people credit for,
just ask them at the time what they are most experienced in, are
best at, or enjoy doing – and they'll tell you! If that happens to
be the thing you want to control, just keep asking until they
give you something you can use.

---

### DO THIS

Answer these questions in order. Don't move on to the next
question until you've answered the previous one. Out loud or in
your head. You don't have to write anything down. Answer in

full – don't be too concise. Apart from question 1, that is. Just your name will do.

1. Hi, what's your name?

2. What do you do for a living?

3. Really? So what's a typical day at work for you then?

4. That sounds all right. You like it there, do you?

5. What else do you have to do?

How was that for you? How did you feel? It was all about you, right? You may have found that you thought about your job in a fresh way. It's nice to be asked questions about yourself. How much did you tell me about your typical day, and what you do? I bet you covered a fair bit of ground there. And I bet that by the time you got to the end of your answer to the last question, you'd started justifying your role to me. Instead of just telling me what you do and how you do it, you moved on to telling me why you're in your job and why your employer needs you. You justified your position. You probably felt like you needed to make your working day sound jam-packed and your role important. You may have even touched on what you're particularly good at in your job, and what you've achieved so far, despite the fact that I didn't ask you. Just by answering those questions, you thought I was paying you some welcome attention. In fact, all the time you were handing more and more of the balance of power to me because you were beginning to *justify* your job instead of *explaining* it. If you and I were face to face, we could have kept going and I could have used some of the stuff in your answers to ask you more questions and force you onto the back foot even more.

Now that you've done that, do this.

---

**DO THIS**

You've just answered these questions yourself. Now it's your turn to ask them. Pick someone you know, but don't tell them what you're doing. Not your best friend or family – someone you can question about their job because you really don't know all the answers. It might even be someone you don't know at all, but end up talking to for some reason.

Ask them these questions. In order. Make sure you've got connection first (see chapter 9), of course. And do a bit of chitchat first, rather than charging straight in.

- What do you do for a living?

- Really? So what's a typical day at work for you, then?

- That sounds all right. You like it there, do you?

- What else do you have to do?

---

When they're answering the last question, they'll probably pause when they think they've run out of info. Important: stay silent! Just wait for them to continue. They will –

they're just searching for the rest of the answer in their unconscious. And it's usually at this point that they will begin to justify themselves.

You'll know when they've begun to justify themselves because they'll start using language like this:

'I also do . . . And . . .'
'I help improve . . .'
'I do . . . because . . .'
'The company needs me to . . .'
'I'm the only one who can . . .'
'I work closely with . . .'
'I'm on the . . . committee.'

While you're listening to their language as they justify themselves, watch their non-verbal signals too. You'll see their face, eyes, head position and all kinds of other stuff change. You'll also feel your connection with them loosen slightly. That's because you're gently pushing them onto the defensive. Don't worry about that. This is what needs to happen for you to gradually take control. You're getting what you want.

> **Remember This**
> *Breaking or loosening connection deliberately is fine, if that's what you've decided to do as part of your plan to get what you want. Getting connection and then taking it away will usually put people on the back foot, unconsciously. It's not the same as losing connection without meaning to. That just means you've lost.*

Once you're fully in charge, you'll notice it go full circle. They will start trying to connect with you. Unconsciously of course, because they probably won't have read this book yet.

However well you end up getting to know this person, never ever tell them you once asked them those questions because you were reading this book to get what you want.

An even easier way of practising this, if you don't think you can remember those questions above, is to wait until the next time you're talking to someone about their job. It happens a lot. It won't be long before it happens again. Once you're chatting, just ask them what they do on a typical day. Let them answer, and then say 'What else?' And then wait until they start justifying themselves as above.

---

**ALERT!** *How to achieve exactly the opposite of what this book is intended to achieve –*

When I first learned this stuff, it was a rocky time for me and my girlfriend. Firing off questions in the style of some sort of interrogation officer is not the way to do it. You can smile, you can nod, you can say 'Really?' or 'OK', while they're answering. Ask the questions – and ask around the questions. Take your time. There's no rush.

---

Remember Sharon (see pages 128–129)? The one with the nice house who was really good at using her celebrity? She was also good at giving *some* credit. Whenever there was someone in her meeting who had experience in a certain field, Sharon would look at them meaningfully and ask 'What do you think about . . . (something that didn't really matter much)?' Sharon would then listen very obviously and intently as she let that person reply in full. The person would leave the meeting feeling valued, listened to, fully in agreement with Sharon's ideas – and wouldn't dream of saying no to her. And then Sharon did exactly what she'd already planned to do anyway – before she'd even got to the meeting.

Giving them *some* credit is a really good technique for getting what you want at work. You can use it outside work, too, if you want to make sure you're in charge of a conversation so you can get what you want. That usually means you need to pay attention to what people tell you about themselves so you can work out what you want to give them some credit for. For example, you can give people credit for being good at sport, watching sport, travelling, cooking or doing DIY; or you can give people credit for having a nice car, house, dress sense, laptop, phone, gadget or joke-telling skills.

I'm older than I was a few years ago. Back then, I quite liked going to the odd nightclub. Especially if I was away on holiday in Ibiza with my mates. When I was on holiday in Ibiza with my girlfriend and *her* mates, I wasn't quite so keen.

Foam was no longer a novelty to me. I regarded it as no more than a soggy pain in the backside. They were keen, though. Keen on going clubbing, that is. It was Friday night. I just fancied going out for some food and then chilling out by the pool with a few beers. And with my girlfriend, of course.

My girlfriend's best mate, Karen, could tell I wanted a quiet one. She got me dancing in that bloody foam again. I have to give her credit for how she did it. She said she wasn't all that well travelled and had only been to Spain once before, when she was small, with her parents. What I didn't know was that my girlfriend had mentioned in the past that I'd travelled around a bit. She chatted away to me about all the places I'd travelled to.

I was a bit of a show-off so I reeled off everything from Alicante and Bruges to Yemen and Zambia. I thought of myself as a seasoned traveller and told her all about where I'd been. And I looked at some pretty damn fine pictures in my mind's eye as I told her my stories. That brought a smile to my face. I told Karen nothing freaked me out and I loved to go somewhere different every time I went away.

She asked me more and more about what my favourite place had been, which country had the best food, where I would go back to if I had the chance, that sort of thing. The more I talked, the more my mind was filled with pictures of my travels. The great feeling of freedom and adventure I have whenever I travel came flooding back. Karen had not only stopped me from making pictures of foam in my mind's eye and dreading the feeling of my soggy shorts and T-shirt clinging to my skin – she'd replaced them with good pictures and feelings instead.

Of course, she didn't really know what she was doing – consciously. This sort of tactic had obviously worked for her more than once when persuading people, and her unconscious had picked it up. It knew the technique, even if she didn't. You'll find that can sometimes be the case with what you're reading in this book. Some people know the odd technique, but don't know they know it.

She asked me if I knew anywhere good to eat in Ibiza town. I'd been there a few times and she said she could tell I liked my food. Of course she could tell, I'd just told her! She asked me to choose where we ate that night, so I did: a good, cheap local place by the harbour near the castle. We went there. We had a brilliant night. The sangria was great, too, and the view was almost as good. I've still got the photos somewhere.

The foam wasn't so bad in the end anyway.

By asking me about my travels, Karen had made me feel good. Without me realizing, she'd also got me to justify my status as the group's most seasoned traveller. I liked Karen for this. I felt we got on well. She'd given me *some* credit – credit for being a traveller and knowing a bit about food. Karen obviously didn't really mind where we ate that evening; she was just focused on getting us all to the foam party afterwards. After the whole group had let me choose the restaurant for the evening – and obviously enjoyed themselves there – I didn't have the heart to say no. Karen had conceded the choice of the restaurant to me. I conceded to her the foam party – what she *really* wanted. That's what giving *some* credit can get you.

I like giving them *some* credit a lot. It's almost my favourite. I love it. Because you can do so many things with it. You can focus on getting something specific from people, or you can use it to be in charge and still have people like you.

---

**DO THIS**

- Think of someone you know who's a bit bossy, overbearing or often critical of you. Put the T-shirt on them. You know what it says. If you don't, see chapter 8.

- Pick something specific about them which doesn't matter to you that you can give them some credit for.

- What are you going to say to give them that credit? How are you going to say it?

- When you do it for real, take a look at their non-verbal signals and how they change. You can tell when it's going down well.

---

Giving them *some* credit usually works best when you're dealing with someone you need to keep on side – but is by nature domineering, pushy, bossy, a bully, loud, or likely to criticize what you do or say. It's usually best to use this technique if you're dealing with someone with whom you have – or want to have – an ongoing relationship.

Giving them *some* credit gives you control and at the same time gets people to like you and therefore cooperate with you. By being the one dishing out the credit, you tell people's unconscious minds that you're in charge. You also make them feel empowered by their own experience, skills or achievements. In truth, you haven't actually empowered them much at all because you've limited the credit you give them to a specific area that doesn't matter to you.

By appearing to defer to them, your suggestion – when it comes – appears to have taken on board their points, and appears to be subject to their agreement even though it's not. The person will feel you have considered their opinion and feel valued. The whole thing will seem to them like you're equal partners. Of course, you're not really. But remember, the credit you give must be genuine.

# 15

# Persuasion Technique Number 6: Breaking Connection

I know it seems a bit odd that I might want to talk to you about the value of breaking connection after we've both made such a big deal of getting connection earlier in the book (see chapter 9). Make no mistake: getting connection alone is far more important and more effective to get what you want. Especially with day-to-day stuff that probably would not develop into any kind of confrontation. It's the kind of stuff that doesn't matter to you in the long term but does make a difference to you at the time.

Breaking connection does play a part, though, sometimes. It buys you time if things aren't going the way you want them to. Breaking connection has two effects. It can get you back the balance of power if you're slightly on the back foot. And it can confuse the other party and throw their autopilots (see pages 41–46) out of sync. Enough so that they pause for a second, and unconsciously give you the chance to take control using one of the other techniques that you've been learning. It buys you time as they unconsciously begin to try to regain connection with you now that they feel they've lost it. Guess who's in charge now.

Here's how you break connection. You do the opposite of getting connection. You read their mood and choose another for yourself. Really get into that new mood – like Meryl Streep (see pages 94–96). It needs to be sufficiently different from theirs so that their unconscious registers that you're breaking connection. So – if they're smiling and happy, you can become impatient and intolerant in your own mind, for example. If they're being all matter of fact and businesslike, you could become overly enthusiastic. Remember – these need to be proper moods with the right pictures and feelings. No play-acting.

Once you've got your mood right, you won't need to bother about much else because everything else will take care of itself. If you want to add a bit of icing on the cake, make sure you fall out of connection non-verbally – with your face and your body – so that you do the opposite to them.

## DO THIS

1. Get connection with someone 'safe' – who you don't really know or you're only talking to temporarily.

2. Practise breaking connection and then getting it again within the same conversation. Watch how they react to you unconsciously – and how they try to regain connection with you once you've broken it. Watch them try to make eye contact, lean in towards

you, take a step towards you. Hear them change their tone and the way they speak. Watch them relax again when you give them their connection back.

Breaking connection confuses or 'throws' the person you want to influence and puts them on the back foot. Once they're there, they'll try to regain connection with you and so become more compliant. While they're trying to get connection back, you can lead the conversation and get them round to your way of thinking using any technique from this book.

# 16

# Hold Them to It

You've almost got what you want. You're so close to getting it that the person you needed to influence has actually said you can have it, or has signalled commitment in some other way. It doesn't stop here. Have you ever agreed to rent or buy a house, and found the other party pulls out even though it was all agreed? It's never a done deal until the keys are in your hand. You know that really.

People are not always as good as their word. That would mean they all had the same rulebook (see chapter 4), wouldn't it? Just because someone tells you they'll do something for you doesn't mean they will. Sometimes you need to stack the odds in your favour even more.

As you know, by a simple process of dehumanization, people can break their word once you're out of their line of sight. For example, 'I know I said you could have a pay rise this autumn but unfortunately the chairman has declared a pay freeze so I'm no longer in a position to give it to you.'

If you think that might happen, or you know that it will –

good. If you think that it won't – bad. You might be right, but you're better off assuming that people are quite likely to go back on their word.

Now that you've followed all the techniques to make it hard to say no, you know how to get commitment from others. Now it's time to maximize on that commitment. That means ensuring it happens, even if it can't happen immediately, and making sure there's little chance of them going back on their word. And making sure that when they do what you want them to do, they do it properly. An added bonus is that once you've done all that, if you want more of it at a later stage, you're more likely to get it.

I'm going to talk to you about IKEA. You've probably already heard a bit about the psychology IKEA uses to get you to spend money. That the floor plan is designed in such a way that, once you're in, you have to walk around more or less the entire store before you get to the checkout. That's obvious – and IKEA does this better than most. But there's a lot more to it than that. IKEA not only secures commitment from you to spend money; it maximizes on that commitment once you're in. The techniques are not exclusive to IKEA and not exclusive to shopping. You can also use them to maximize commitments once you get them. Let's look at how IKEA does it first.

You walk into the store. There's your commitment. You've made the journey (normally a longer journey than you would usually make to go shopping) and you've walked through the door. At some level, consciously or unconsciously, you've already decided to buy something. You might have decided what that is before setting off for IKEA, or you might just have come to IKEA to 'have a look around'. You know that means you're ready to get your credit card out.

Rewind for a second. How did they get you there in the first place? Through their advertising and branding, they've given you *some* credit. Either for having a sense of style, or 'good' taste for clean, modern, contemporary furniture. And they've given you credit for having the ability – however slight – to construct your own furniture. They've even told you the narrow realm of 'good taste' that you have. They've also cleverly turned their downsides into upsides. Think about it. What have their competitors got as an advantage? Answer: ready-built furniture; furniture that you don't have to put together. But that can mean you have to wait a few weeks for delivery. And you'll definitely have to pay for that delivery. So what do IKEA do? They tell you – explicitly – that their products are deliberately flat-packed to enable you to take them home yourself straight away (and if you do – no delivery charge). Plus they'll let you know that flat-packing keeps their costs down, which they pass on to you, the customer. That's how they beat the competition. That's how IKEA get your business. There's more on how you can turn your downsides into upsides in Chapter 17, 'Know Your Enemy'.

But that's only the beginning of the story. Now that you've committed (you're in the store), it's time for IKEA to maximize your commitment. The forward route takes you past most of their products to entice you to spend more than you originally intended before you get to the checkout. If you turn round and go out the way you came in, you'll be doing so against a tide of other people coming in. There are arrows on the floor reinforcing that point – telling you which way you should be walking. And just before you get to the products, there's a children's playpen for your kids to use for free and for as long as they like. To really ram home your commitment, you're invited to pick up a bag, a pencil and a measuring tape. Now you've picked those up, you're not only showing commitment, but you've almost run out of excuses not to buy. IKEA works like this:

- They've persuaded you to give them what they want by giving you *some* credit (see chapter 14).

- They've made it difficult for you to back out of that commitment, now that you're in the store. Both physically and mentally in this case. They've made you feel (potentially) bad.

- They've reinforced your commitment. In this case by having you pick up the bag, the measuring tape and the pencil. Now your autopilots (see pages 41–46) have got you automatically assuming you're going to walk out with something. You're also making pictures in your mind of the finished product and what it will look like in your home. The store is helpfully kitted out with furniture that's already been put together so that you're sufficiently distracted from the process of putting it together.

- Now they give you something that's 'over and above' (see pages 203–207) – and before you've done your part of the deal. In this case they give you a children's playpen. You could probably argue that – in theory at least – it's free. But if you meet someone who's ever gone to IKEA, allowed their kids to play in the pen, and then walked straight out, tell them to give me a call. I'd love to get inside their head and copy a few of their autopilots for myself.

That's how IKEA do it and they're highly successful. And they have a great product. My house is full of IKEA stuff. But, of course, you're not a global multi-billion-krona furniture chain, are you? To maximize getting what you want, you just need to do the same things, slightly differently.

Here's what you do:

- You persuade them – you know how. Use one or more persuasion techniques.

- You make them feel bad about backing out.

- You reinforce their commitment.

- You give them something that's 'over and above' and before they've done what you want them to do. You strike first, in other words.

## Make them feel bad

To start with, I'm going to make you feel bad (briefly!). I'm going to try to make you feel bad about eating junk food.

If you eat healthily and stay away from junk food, you'll feel better, be healthier and probably live for longer. Eating good food will set up some brand-new autopilots that make you look forward to eating healthily. If you do eat junk food in moderation, it will still have a negative effect. You should eat healthily all the time.

*OK, my turn.*

*If you eat unhealthily – or too much junk food – you will feel worse, you will see your health suffer and people will tell you you're getting fat. You'll probably die sooner, too. Eating junk food will set up some brand-new autopilots that make you feel hungry for junk rather than healthy food. If you do eat healthy food in moderation, it will still have a positive effect. If you walk past a burger bar, look in the opposite direction.*

I don't need to tell you which one's more effective. Most people are influenced more easily if you show them how *bad* it might be if they *don't* do something. Rather than how *good* it might be if they *do* it. Instinct tells you how to behave to ensure that you *don't* die.

That's why cigarette packets often now show graphic pictures of people with hideous smoking-related diseases, tar-stained lungs and the like. And it's why most people prefer to avoid confrontation – because they fear what might happen if they do take someone on face to face. I am more likely to get what I want from you if I get you to fear the consequences of not doing it, than if I get you to look forward to the benefits of doing it.

If I were your parent and wanted to stop you from climbing trees, which would work best? Telling you that you might break your neck and end up in a wheelchair for the rest of your life if you fall? Or telling you it's better to make sure you keep both feet on the ground so you can continue to walk on them for the rest of your life?

Or, if I want you to quit smoking, should I tell you that you might die a long, lingering and painful death if you don't? Or that you'll be happy and healthy for longer if you do? (I should say here that smoking is a physical and mental addiction so it takes more than just a form of words to get someone to quit and become healthy. It's still much easier than most people will have you believe, though; you just need to think about it in the right way. And, of course, if you decide it's going to be difficult, it will be.)

And if I tell you that being on good terms with everyone all the time will make your life easier, it's true. But it's nowhere near as powerful as saying that you shouldn't have arguments, because they can make you unpopular, get you fired or even beaten up.

OK, that's stages 1 and 2 done – the persuasion part and the part where you make them feel bad. Before we do stages 3 and 4 – reinforcing their commitment and going over and above – you need to do this.

---

### DO THIS

- Think of something you feel you want to do, or you must do, but for some reason you don't do.

- What benefits would you get if you did this thing?

- How bad will it be if you don't?

---

Unless you can answer all three questions above, you probably won't persuade yourself to do it. The same goes for the person you want to influence.

---

**DO THIS**

- Think of what you want them to do.
- What benefits are there for them if they do it?
- How bad will it be for them if they don't?

---

It's the third question that people often forget to ask themselves – and forget to point out.

Once you've worked out how bad it will be for them if they don't, there's a knack to how you point it out to them. The reason it was more effective for me to talk about you *seeing* your health suffer, people *telling* you you're getting fat and *feeling* hungry for junk is because I painted a picture, with sounds and feelings. I took charge of the pictures that you make in your mind – and influenced your internal dialogue – with just my words.

Like this:

You're standing by a pool, in your swimming costume, in a hot country. You need to jump in – it's too hot out here. You can't take any more.

or:

It's baking hot. You can feel the relentless red heat of the sun beating down on your head and body. The air is still and close. There's no breeze. You see the heat radiating upwards from the cracked, brown earth all around you. You'll be in pain for days if you don't get out of the sun.

Go back to the last 'Do This'. Now do it again. This time, 'paint the pain' – in pictures, feelings and sounds. Make it vivid.

When you're painting pain for the person you want to influence, it's good to say it using 'Do it without quotes', featured in Chapter 11. For example, if you want to let someone know that not paying their fair share of the bill in a restaurant would really annoy you and your friends, you could mention someone you know who is constantly talked about behind their back for not paying their fair share.

## Reinforce with pictures

Like IKEA, you know how to persuade them and you know how to make them feel bad if they don't do what they say they'll do. You reinforce their commitment and get them to imagine doing whatever you're holding them to. You ask them when they're going to do it, where they're going to do it and how. The more detail you get from them at this point, the better. Make sure that as you reinforce, you create pictures in their head of them doing what they've said they'll do.

So if someone at work has agreed to finish a project by Thursday, ask them 'What time on Thursday will you have it done by? Where will you be while you're finishing it? And how are you going to let me know when it's done?' This should get them seeing in their mind's eye things like their desk, maybe even a picture of themselves sitting at the desk, their computer and so on. Plus they will probably also envisage themselves picking up the phone, or sending an email, to let you know that it's done. They may even see the office clock on the wall showing the time that they've decided to get it done by.

If it's easier, and you don't want to ask – just tell them when, where and how. They'll still make their own pictures based on your words. For example, say something like: 'So I guess you'll have that done by the end of the week. You just need to speak to your boss to get the go-ahead when you're over at head office.' You know the sort of thing I mean.

Here's another example. Let's say you want to move in with your partner. Your partner's agreed to talk about it and you want to make sure the conversation happens and doesn't just get pushed to one side. Get your partner picturing when, where and how you'll be having that conversation. Say, 'Let's talk about that on Wednesday night at my place over dinner. I'll cook spaghetti Bolognese.' Give that sort of detail.

If someone's agreed to join you on your new fitness regime, say something like, 'OK, so put next Monday evening at 7 p.m. in your diary. We'll go to Virgin Active in Chelmsford in my car. I'll pick you up at your place.' Specific, you see.

Getting people to picture internally what you want them to do makes them much more likely to do it. Particularly if they're actually doing it in their mind's eye. When people do this, the brain finds it difficult to distinguish between stuff that really happens and stuff it imagines happening. So if you can get someone to imagine doing a particular thing in the near future, their brain will make an unconscious assumption that they've already started to do it for real. It's a way of getting people used to new ideas before they put them into practice.

## Over and above

The final stage is to give them something 'Over and above' what they're expecting from you – and before they've done their bit. Like the playpen in IKEA.

A couple of stories. The first one shows you how just doing something 'over and above' – but striking *first* – can almost literally have people eating out of your hand.

Grant is a laid-back kind of bloke. He usually does what he likes. At work and at home. In the office, he's on Facebook all the time, texts his mates, is always laughing and joking – and does anything, really, apart from any work. How does his boss, Marie, let him get away with it? How come he's so popular with everyone even though they have to do most of his work for him? Answer: he brings biscuits. At the start of the day. Not just any biscuits. I mean those big, soft, chewy, double chocolate biscuits. There are those pictures again. Did that get your mouth watering? When Grant doesn't want to do anything at work on a given day, he brings biscuits. That's what happens when you strike first and go 'over and above'.

The next story begins with a question. Would you let me come round to your house and take your floorboards up? And would you then let me remove the panel from the side of your bath? Would you let me and my family come round every morning just before you left for work and every evening as soon as you got home? For a week? Would you let me leave random pieces of salad and cheese around your bathroom floor and your hallway once I'd done all that with your floorboards, bath panel, and so on? Would you let me sleep overnight in your bathroom on the floor? To cap it all, would you let me do all this if you didn't own your property, and you knew your landlord made a habit of dropping by unannounced to check that everything's OK? Would you let me bring my dad along, and take him straight up to the bathroom in tears? Would you let me drill random holes in the walls of your bathroom and hallway? Would you behave as if you were wearing a T-shirt that said, 'I've been a mug before, so I can be a mug again.' Would you?

My brother did.

It all started with a holiday and a small favour. The Kerry family lived nearby and they were off on their usual trip to Portugal for a week. My brother's son, Andrew, was friends with their son, Martin. Martin had a goldfish and a hamster that he wanted Andrew to look after while he was away. My brother and his wife said that was fine and Mr and Mrs Kerry popped over one evening with Martin to drop off Hercules the hamster (or Herc, for short) and Peter the goldfish.

And a flowery pot plant.

Martin's mum gave Andrew's mum a sheet of paper with instructions on how to look after Herc and Peter – and a thank-you note that she'd written in advance. 'Don't thank me, yet,' said my sister-in-law, 'thank me when you get back!'

It's day two in the little hamster house. The door is open and Herc has done a runner. He's still alive, though. They know this because they've been woken up at 3 a.m. two nights in a row. By the burglar alarm. The first night, the alarm sounded because the motion sensors in the hallway were a bit oversensitive and could even detect a small rodent. On the second night, the alarm went off because Herc got a bit peckish and decided to help himself to a portion of burglar alarm cable.

My brother tried everything. Exhausted as he was, he went to the pet shop for expert advice on how to recapture Herc, who was having a whale of a time under the floorboards, gnawing, scratching and chewing. My brother never paid much attention at school but it was at this point – aged 35 – that he learned the well-known fact that hamsters are nocturnal.

Despite a network of humane traps and devices, by the time the Kerry family got back from their 'very relaxing' break in the Algarve, Herc was still at large in his new subterranean home, under my brother's bathroom.

Martin started crying. Mrs Kerry looked as if she might keel over. Mr Kerry's eyes welled up and glazed over. Later that evening, Martin's grandparents also joined the search and rescue operation for Herc.

My sister-in-law made them tea as she – albeit reluctantly – stood by as they dug up the first of her floorboards. As efforts to recover Herc intensified and a 24-hour toll-free missing hamster hotline was set up (OK, I'm overdoing it here, I know), off came the bath panel. And although I was joking about the hotline, they really did call the house about every 10 minutes to see if Herc had come out!

After a few days of intensive digging and dismantling, not to mention the various bits of ham, cheese, carrot and lettuce spread around that were now beginning to smell a bit, came the final straw. My sister-in-law apologized but said she was not able to grant Mrs Kerry's request to camp out in the bathroom overnight, in case Herc surfaced under cover of darkness. Not even when Mrs Kerry explained that she had hired a set of thermal imaging goggles as the latest hi-tech addition to the 'Find Herc' campaign. And no I'm not joking.

To the best of my knowledge, Herc is still AWOL. Missing in action. The Kerry family are coming to terms with their tragic loss now that they've bought Zeus. Herc may be gone, but his spirit lives on. My rulebook says I'd have gone straight to the pet shop to buy a Herc clone, so nobody was any the wiser, thus shielding me and my family from two sleepless nights, two days without a wash, hundreds of pounds worth of home repairs and a humiliating letter from the landlord.

Here's what happened in my brother and sister-in-law's unconscious minds, which caused them to allow the Kerry family to dismantle their home. Firstly, they got commitment from my brother and his wife to look after the pets. Simple connection got them that – nothing more needed – persuasion done.

It was obvious that the whole family loved Herc. He had a lovely cage and lots of toys – and they *all* came to drop him and Peter the fish off. Would anybody feel bad if something went wrong? You bet.

A detailed set of instructions came with Herc and Peter – telling my brother et al how and when to feed them, clean them out and all the rest of it. Commitment reinforced: take good care of Herc and Peter.

And finally they gave my sister-in-law something 'over and above' before she'd done her bit. The pot plant and the thank-you note came at the beginning.

Look at what my family were willing to do to keep their side of the bargain. They were prepared to go to ridiculous lengths to return him to the Kerry family safe and sound. They allowed the Kerry family to wreck their home!

---

**DO THIS**

- Think of something someone has already agreed to do for you (it doesn't matter whether you had to use a technique to get their agreement for this).

- What would be the downside for them of not doing it?

- Paint the pain to them – preferably delivered in the third person.

- Reinforce the commitment – with 'when' and 'how'.

- Give them something 'over and above' before they've given you what they want (remember they've already committed). Or do something for them that's 'over and above'.

---

'Holding them to it' is used after you've persuaded somebody by 'Getting connection', 'Using your celebrity', 'Being human or inhuman', 'Giving them *some* credit' or 'Breaking connection'. You need to 'Hold them to it' because people can go back on their word even after you've persuaded them successfully.

You use 'Holding them to it' to maximize their level of commitment. There are three stages to this once you've persuaded them successfully:

- Make them feel bad by painting a negative picture of what will happen if they don't comply.

- Reinforce their commitment by asking when they'll do it, where and how.

- Then give them something in return – in advance. Make sure it's 'Over and above' what they would expect. And make sure you strike first.

# 17

# Know Your Enemy

You know all about successful people. Successful people have good autopilots (see pages 41–46) like yours. They keep doing the right thing and they stop doing the wrong thing. You'll also find that successful people are highly likely to be good at persuasion. Which means they'll have inadvertently picked up some of the stuff you've been reading in this book – only they won't really know what they've picked up because it's sitting in the unconscious part of their brain. The bit that does things automatically. They'll probably be using this kind of material simply because on some level their brain has registered that it's been successful in the past.

The fact that these people are using these persuasion techniques unconsciously probably means they're using them well. But they're almost certainly not using them all.

This section is all about what to do if you come up against people using these techniques. Perhaps they've struck first, and you haven't had time to plan your approach.

**Remember This**

*Ideally, getting what you want means you have to plan ahead. But you can't always.*

You might not have time to plan but you'll recognize the techniques when they come and you'll know how to stop someone getting what they want from you. The fact that you know what they're doing means you're in charge already.

By recognizing their technique, you'll see quickly what they're trying to get from you. That immediately defuses the power of the technique. Imagine if you knew how Houdini did it. Your astonishment at his skills would wane immediately. Knowing their technique, and what they're trying to get, means you are now in control. You can give them what they want (knowingly!), if that's OK with you. Or you can *not* give them what they want. Or you can come up with something new that would make you both happy. Or something new that would make just you happy. It's your choice.

If you really don't want to give them what they want, however much they try, then it's easy: just hold the thought. Just decide that not only do you not want to give them what they want, but if necessary, you'll give them the opposite – 100 per cent the opposite. If anyone – you or them – has already decided to do the complete opposite, then no amount of persuading is going to work. Most people are persuadable most of the time. Remember, they've got the T-shirt (see chapter 8), and they're wearing it: 'I've been persuaded before. And I can be persuaded again . . . and again . . . and again'. But not if they've already decided to do the complete opposite.

So if someone's trying to get money from you for some

reason and you really don't want to give them any – however persuasive they are – then just decide to do the opposite: decide to get money from them. Let's say I'm trying to sell you something and I'm making a really good case. You actually start to think that you might want the thing I'm selling. But you really don't want to part with any money.

All you do to neutralize me is decide that rather than thinking about whether you should buy from me, you decide you'd like to sell *me* something instead. What could you sell me? A product? A service? Or something you own that I might like? You don't even have to say it. You just need to think about it in that way and you will isolate yourself from any powers of persuasion, however good they are. Well, almost any. But that's another story.

While I'm at it, you may come across people who have – for some reason – already decided, 100 per cent, to give you the opposite of what you want. You might want to go out with them, but they may have decided to go out with someone else. You may go for a job interview where the company has already decided to give the job to someone else. Or you may try to give a relationship one last try with someone who has already decided to leave you for someone else. You see – it has to be the opposite for them to be totally unpersuadable. That's not the same as someone who thinks they've decided, 100 per cent, *not* to give you what you want. Not at all. You can persuade them still.

And it doesn't really matter even if you *do* come up against someone who has already decided, 100 per cent, to do the opposite of what you want. You're adaptable. You know there are other ways of getting what you want. Who is the next most important person you need to convince now?

## Liar, liar

You know all about rulebooks (see chapter 4). Sometimes you'll meet people who mean well, but just have different rulebooks from yours. And at other times you're going to encounter people who are out to get you. Really out to get you. The kind of people who lie and cheat their way through life regardless of the impact on other people. I'm not talking about people who are overtly and obviously shits. They're easy; you can spot them a mile off. I'm talking about those who say they're your friend, but are not.

Ninety-nine per cent of the time, your unconscious will tell you when someone's not what they seem. It's almost always right. It's commonly known as your gut feeling and you know how that works and why you should listen to it. The problem is that if you think someone's your friend or on your side, you won't *want* to listen to your gut when it warns you off. So you'll ignore it. Even though you know, deep down, that something – or someone – is not right. So I'm going to show you how to use your *conscious* brain to check for enemies.

A quick word about brain filters. Here's how you set them. The next time you go out, do some car spotting. As an example, check to see how many Minis there are on the road. You'll see Minis all over the place. Many more than you expected. There aren't more, of course, it's just that you have set your brain to spot them. Your conscious brain can't cope with the millions of bits of info it takes in through your five senses every second. It has to filter. It puts what it thinks is important to you into your *conscious* so you can take notice of it, and it puts all the rest into your unconscious, which processes it all in the background without making a fuss about it. If you *tell* your brain what you want it to put into your conscious – i.e. what's important to you – it will obey you. So, tell it to look out for Minis, and you'll see many Minis. Tell it to look out for people smoking and you'll see far more people smoking than you expect. Tell it to listen out for a particular song on the radio, and you'll hear nothing but that song. Not all filters are useful. If you put your brain on alert for illnesses, aches and pains, you'll start to feel them. So don't do that.

Here's the filter you need in order to know your enemy. It's called, not surprisingly, the enemy filter. If there's a chance that someone might be trying to screw you over, just a chance, but you're not sure, then the enemy filter will reveal this. And even when you've put it on and worked out that someone's fine, put it on again at a later date just to be sure. People can change. A friend of mine has even created a second T-shirt to help him with this. He makes sure that – when necessary – he has people wearing one saying 'I might be your friend, but I could be your enemy'. You may find that technique useful now – or later, once you've digested this book in full.

## DO THIS

Write each answer down – or say it out loud if you like. Don't just answer in your head.

- Think about someone you know – anyone for now.

- Imagine they were trying to screw you over. What would they be doing and how would they be doing it? What might they want from you?

- Now that you're thinking about it, do you tend to make/have you tended to make excuses for them? Usually this includes the words 'Oh he/she is just . . .' or 'He/she is only . . .' 'That's just the way he/she is.' 'He's just drunk.' 'She's just got a lot on her plate.' 'He's just new.' 'She's just a bit insecure.' 'He's just joking.'

- Imagine a friend of yours telling you what they – not you – think what *they* think – about this person. What would they say?

- Find a friend you trust who doesn't know this person – not necessarily the one above – and tell them what you've just told me. Ask them what they think. Is this person an enemy?

Now that you've done this, you should know what your gut feeling was all along. Is this person an enemy? If not, great. Do this again in a few months' time just to make sure. If yes, then well done. You're in charge already. It's up to you what you do now.

This is the way you expose your gut feeling if you haven't

noticed what it's been saying. Otherwise you would end up doing what most people do most of the time. You would notice what your gut *had* been saying all along, once it was too late. Hindsight is a wonderful thing but it doesn't help much. Foresight is better.

Remember – now that you know the enemy filter, you can reapply it whenever you want to. But, the most important thing to remember is that you must assume *anyone* can be your enemy. Just because you don't *want* them to be an enemy doesn't mean they're not. And you know already that if you want them to be squeaky clean, you'll choose to see them as that even if they're not. And that will mean you'll ignore your gut feeling if it tells you something is wrong. And you know that ignoring your gut will definitely not get you what you want.

While I'm talking about liars, I could go on forever about how to spot one when they're staring you in the face. Although you might not need this now, I'll share a few secrets with you anyway. Despite what people might tell you, there's no such thing as a Pinocchio's nose, no universal way of telling when people are lying. If you think about rulebooks, then it stands to reason that some people will be extremely comfortable with telling lies and others will be uncomfortable if they have to lie for some reason. And that means they'll feel differently about what they're doing – and that will be displayed differently in the way they communicate with you. But, there are some rules of thumb.

The pitch of someone's voice will often go up when they're not telling the truth. Their blink rate will also probably change – it will speed up or slow down. If you're close enough to see into their eyes, their pupils will usually dilate. If they shake their head while they're saying 'Yes', they probably mean no. And if they say 'No, YEAH . . .' or 'yeah, NO' – they usually mean the word they said first.

There's a lot of other stuff too – like fidgeting, looking up and to the side, not making eye contact, licking lips, etc. There's truth in all of them – but they're not reliable because there are so many other possible causes for them. For example, you probably fidget when you're nervous. You'd perhaps fidget, possibly lick your lips, and sweat, and your eyes would dart all over the place, if you were being questioned by the police. Even if you were innocent.

I know all that's true, but I don't bother with the conscious stuff. I know the best way of spotting a liar is to listen to my gut.

## The red button

We've saved this one until last. It's called the Red Button because it's your last resort. You only press the Red Button when nothing else has worked and the **** is about to hit the fan. I hope you never have to use the Red Button because my rulebook really doesn't like it very much. I hope yours is simi-lar to mine in that respect. Whether we like it or not, you need to know the Red Button technique because people might use it against you. And you may find yourself in a position where you have no option but to use it back.

Press the Red Button when someone else is trying to shaft you big time.

Let's just talk about some other people for a second. You

know most people's rulebooks are different from yours in some way. Some people's are so different that they'll do absolutely anything to get what they want – and go head to head with you, whether you know it or not. That puts you into direct competition, whether you like it or not. You know already that the winner of any competition is usually the person who can be the most adaptable most quickly. The Red Button is there so that if you need it, you can make sure it's you – and not them.

You might want to use it if:

- Someone's trying to steal your bloke.

- Another bloke is flirting with your girlfriend.

- Someone at work is plotting to get you fired.

- Someone's trying to freeze you out of your group.

- Someone's spreading malicious gossip about you.

- A rival company is attempting to scupper your chances of winning a deal.

- Someone has launched a dirty tricks campaign against you.

Before you go near the Red Button, you need to choose the right belief. Just like when you visualize the T-shirt (see chapter 8). There have been times in my life when I've taken a look at whoever I'm up against and thought 'What's the point? I might as well give up now.'

Sometimes I tried to fight back – but only half-heartedly. I would convince myself to give it a go, that I might get lucky one time. But it didn't pay off because the competition was too great – and I knew it. Deep down, I knew I had no chance anyway. My internal dialogue (see pages 19–23) was really helpful in those days. Not.

Here's the first step. You need to decide at what point you're going to say to yourself 'Right, enough is enough. I need to fight back.' People have different thresholds.

So what's your threshold? If something's not going well, how long does it take you to say 'That's it. I've had enough of this. I need to take urgent action.'? Knowing your threshold is a good thing. For some people it's really quick – after one or two setbacks. Others say 'never again' after just one. Some take a long time before they decide enough is enough.

A person can smoke thousands of cigarettes for years before they say 'That's it, it's time to stop killing myself and think about being healthier.' And some endure years of hurt before they realize they're in the wrong relationship. Then there are those who eat and drink badly until they're so uncomfortable with their size and appearance that it dawns on them they are doing something wrong, and the thing they thought was giving them 'comfort' is actually the cause of their pain.

As I write this, the world's fattest man is Manuel Uribe, from Mexico. At his heaviest, aged 42, he weighed 89 stone. That's 571 kilogrammes. Or 1257 pounds. Or just over half a tonne. Manuel was bedridden for five years. When the moment finally came for him to go to hospital, he had to be winched out of his bedroom window and loaded onto a flatbed lorry with a crane.

At what point do you think Manuel decided he'd put on a

bit too much weight? When he found himself out of breath at the top of the stairs? Or when he had to buy new clothes because the old ones didn't fit? When he had to have his clothes specially made? When he couldn't get out of his front door to see his doctor? Or he found himself in the newspapers? Or when he needed help to go to the toilet (thank God he didn't have my bladder)?

I know you're thinking, 'I would never have let it get that far.' You're thinking that you would have done something about it a lot sooner. Some people would have taken action when they found themselves loosening their belt one notch. You may sit somewhere on that scale – between them and Manuel.

Manuel is an extreme case, of course. What's your threshold? How far do things have to go before you've had enough? How big would you need to get? How miserable would you need to become? How poor would you need to be? How addicted? How depressed? How unsuccessful? How many times do you need to be shafted by people with very different rulebooks before you decide to do something?

Here's how you know when it's time to take action:

- Your internal dialogue talks of nothing but this problem.

- You're feeling anxious, down or angry about it.

- It's the first thing you think of when you wake up or the last thing you think of when you go to sleep.

- You may be having trouble sleeping or feel ill.

- Or you'll just know you've had enough.

When a big problem like this comes up, some people give up. Others tackle it head-on. If you've been giving up until now, I'm going to show you how to tackle it head-on. If you're already that sort of person, this is how to get even better at it.

If your internal dialogue has ever told you something was a lost cause, it was wrong – it wasn't. If it's ever told you there was no chance of standing up for yourself, there was. If you thought you were way out of someone's league, you aren't. As you know, most of the time you'll end up believing what your internal dialogue (see pages 19–23) tells you. And you know how to change your internal dialogue now.

The key to fighting back is to create doubt. Doubt in the mind of the person or people that matter. Not the person trying to shaft you – but the person they're trying influence to your detriment. Let's imagine a colleague of yours, Jack, is trying to get you sacked by blaming you for all kinds of things whenever he talks to the boss. You need to create doubt in the boss's mind about Jack.

When I say doubt, I don't mean any old doubt. The doubt you create must be about the very thing the boss thinks is *great* about Jack. So much so that the boss begins seeing that as a downside, not an upside. Once you've done that, you use a similar technique to demonstrate subtly what's great about you.

Rather than creating doubt about Jack by focusing on his weak points (that's obvious – anyone can do that), you do it by focusing on his strong points. You hit the boss right where his autopilots are not expecting it. Think about it. If the boss is in any way prepared for you to fight back against Jack (and that's a big 'if'), his autopilots will not be ready for you. They'll be waiting for you to focus on Jack's *weak* points.

Here's what I mean.

I like Liam. He's a hard worker, a perfectionist and a really outgoing and funny bloke.

True, but that can mean he's stressed out a lot, a bit of a slavedriver and too keen on the sound of his own voice.

I hadn't thought about it like that.

Catherine is experienced, knowledgeable and honest. But that can mean she's been in the job too long, sometimes can't see the wood for the trees and can be a bit insensitive at times. Or it could mean she's done lots of jobs – each one not for very long, is sometimes reluctant to learn new things and doesn't toe the company line.

Damian is a great dad, does lots of interesting things in his spare time and cares about the environment. But that can mean he's under the thumb at home, doesn't stick at things for long and has a tendency to go on and on about global warming.

Jim's such good company. He's really laid-back, has loads of friends and always puts me completely at ease when I'm with him. But that can mean things never get done, he's fickle and highly manipulative. He's generous to a fault. But that can mean he's prone to buy the odd favour.

Getting it? Good. Your turn.

Ross is good-looking and rich. What can that mean, do you think? I guess it can mean that he's ruthless, he loves himself a bit too much and he's materialistic. It might not necessarily, but it can – can't it?

What about Deborah? She's kind, helpful and friendly. But that can mean . . .?

That she's false, needy and insincere? Or . . .?

---

**DO THIS**

- Think of someone you know but don't trust.

- Think of three qualities about them that most people would recognize.

- Now come up with three interpretations of those qualities that are negative.

---

Don't worry if not everyone is likely to agree with your negative interpretation of someone's 'qualities'. Just sowing the seed of an idea that perhaps there's a flipside to the coin is enough

---

**ALERT! *How to Achieve Exactly the Opposite of What This Book is Intended to Achieve –***

You reserve the Red Button for when you're really up against it and you've tried everything else. If you're genuinely defending your corner, most people would respect you for it. If you just start pressing it for the hell of it, there's a high risk you'll come across as a catty, back-biting sneak.

to get their internal dialogue voicing doubts to them. As you know, once their internal dialogue starts saying something new, it'll start the process of creating new beliefs in their head; beliefs about Jack – or whoever is trying to screw you – which will make them look bad, not you.

Here are a few to start you off but the list goes on. It gets easier the more you do it:

A good listener – nosey?

Always sees the big picture – no attention to detail?

Always smartly dressed – self-absorbed?

Ambitious – ruthless?

Detailed – can't see the wood for the trees?

Down to earth – crass?

Driven – inconsiderate?

Expert – narrow field of know-how?

Extrovert – annoying show-off?

Fair-minded – unwilling to commit?

Good at problem-solving – always looking for problems?

Has good taste – snobbish?

Has nice things – insecure?

Has the common touch – patronizing?

Reliable – dull?

Self-starter – not a team player?

Sporty – smug?

Talented – complacent?

Team player – shy of accountability?

Trusting – naive?

Well read – introverted?

It's worth making the point that these 'equivalents' are not always the case. Depending on the individual, you might come up with your own. The most important thing is to exercise your mind so you can start seeing people's apparent qualities in a different way.

Now that you're able to convert upsides into downsides, it's all about how you deliver that information to the person you want to influence. Here are a few examples of how to be convincing. I'll explain the techniques a bit more once you've read them.

My cousin is a psychiatrist. She says most people who are told they're mentally ill, aren't. Well not at first. She says if someone is told something enough times, they will begin to believe it – and *make* it true, whether or not it was true in the first place. You already know about beliefs and how you can form them based on your experiences, so this won't surprise you at all.

I was reading the newspaper on Sunday and there was an

article saying there was now proof that a doctor's bedside manner has a direct impact on a patient's recovery rates.

A friend of mine is Spanish. He's lived in Manchester for five years and now speaks brilliant English. He says he was never any good at languages at school so if he can learn to speak a foreign language fluently, anyone can.

I know a Human Resources manager. She says that people who rise through the ranks of one company over a period of time tend to be afraid of change and often end up promoted to a level beyond their abilities.

My brother runs a bar. He says people who order champagne as a matter of course (rather than for a celebration) often behave badly and get thrown out.

I saw on the News the other night that doctors now reckon playing lots of video games can lead to impotence.

I want to go to Thailand this year because I love the food. My mates fancied something different and more adventurous. They wanted to give Cambodia a try. I told them I'd watched the Travel Channel and it said that Cambodia was risky and the experts had said many travellers had found it to be an expensive mistake.

OK, I'll come clean. It's all about the third person. You might remember it from Chapter 11 called 'Do it without quotes'. You attribute the message to someone else – so it's not actually coming directly from you. If it looked like your own message, you'd come across as having an interest or your own agenda. If, though, you appear to be delivering someone else's message, it adds an air of authority and credibility to that message while distancing you from the source. If you can add an element of celebrity to your 'source' of information, all the better. For example, if it comes from an expert, someone who wears a uniform, a white coat, a badge, a high-visibility jacket – that sort of thing. Or the TV, the news, the Internet, newspapers, books, etc. If you can't, don't worry. Just attributing it to a third party works almost as well.

This principle of using the third person in reported speech comes from the widely respected work carried out by a group of eminent psychologists in Pennsylvania in 2007.

No it doesn't. But you see what I mean. It had a great influence on you for a moment.

I've been on the receiving end of this technique. I was in my early twenties and I really fancied a woman at work. I was sure she fancied me, too. We were at a work do one evening and had been talking for ages. One of the sales reps then began to make an approach to her. I was fit at the time, as in physically fit. I had muscles and bulges and everything. I'll admit now that I bought my shirts a size too small to show it all off. Obviously, nowadays, a size too big works much better for me. Adaptable, you see.

This sales rep, Greg, destroyed my muscles in front of me. He said to Gemma: 'No wonder he's got those biceps. My mate goes to the same gym and he says he's in there five nights a week and at weekends!' Then he turned to me, grinning, in front of Gemma and asked me in a jokey way if I actually had a life. I found myself justifying my gym routine to him, which won't surprise you because you know all about people justifying themselves already. Gemma must have thought I was a right loser. I gave up on Gemma after that.

---

## DO THIS

- Identify someone – or something – who might have it in for you.

- Take three upsides of their personality or ability – and turn them into downsides.

- Decide where your third-party information would 'come from' if you were doing it for real. For example – a friend, an expert, a website, a 'source' of some kind. Maybe even the TV.

- Practise what you would say '_ _ _ _ _ _ BUT that can mean/BUT some people say/BUT I read somewhere that _ _ _ _ _ _' and attribute it to your source.

- Don't press the Red Button. That was just for practice, in case you ever need it.

---

You'll remember what the word 'but' does (see page 118). It makes a person forget what comes before it and only remember what comes after it.

So if you really need to mention someone's qualities when using this technique, make sure you mention them before the word 'but' and then launch into the downsides that you have created from them after that.

Now that you've finished learning this technique, I'll share one last thing with you. You can use it in reverse – to turn your own downsides into upsides. To make sure you fight back as well as you can.

If you're regarded as a bit bossy, perhaps that means you manage projects well? Or you're a natural leader? If you're known as a bit shy, could that mean you think and reflect on things – a good person to consult for a considered opinion? And obviously, you would never let your ego get in the way of a good decision, would you? If people complain that you don't let them get a word in edgeways, I wonder if it's crossed their mind that you might be worth listening to? Drink too much – good for a laugh? Not career-minded – stress free? Overly fussy – quality matters? Overbearing – highly confident? Too emotional – a big heart?

## Conclusion

The Red Button is your nuclear option. Smash glass and use only in an emergency. It works by turning someone's strengths into weaknesses and then delivering that information as if it's being reported in the third person – i.e. not coming from you. Delivering information from a third party works by informing the other person's unconscious mind that you have no agenda and lends credibility to what you're saying. Using the third person is a technique widely used by hypnotherapists while their patients are in a deep trance. We have adapted it for use in everyday life. No trance needed.

If the third party – the apparent source of information –

happens to have a level of celebrity (i.e. authority or expertise), this technique works even better.

As a final twist, you can add to it by turning your own weaknesses into strengths by applying the same process in reverse.

# 18

# Your New Autopilots

Take a look at the next successful person you meet and see how many techniques you can spot. When I say successful, I mean it in the broadest sense. They could be successful at work, in their personal life or with people generally. They could even be one of those people who just seem to have all the luck. You'll definitely find that they're using one or more of these kinds of techniques to get what they want, unconsciously of course. The way it will have worked for them is that the unconscious part of their brain will have remembered when certain ways of behaving got them what they wanted. It will then have developed a habit of repeating those behaviours and, you know this already, a successful autopilot will have started running in the background so that they could be successful – and do successful things – time and time again. Without really realizing.

Let me mention success for a second. Thinking and behaving successfully doesn't come naturally to everyone. A lot depends on the autopilots that were formed based on your experiences when you were young. The good news, as you know, is that even if it doesn't come naturally, everyone can change their autopilots if theirs are not as successful as other people's. You just need to take notice of how you're reacting and behaving in a certain situation. If you're not being successful, then you need to practise changing that reaction, which will start creating a new autopilot to replace the old one.

One of the hallmarks of a successful person is their ability to stick with things that work and ditch the things that don't. I know that might sound obvious but you'd be surprised. How many people do you know who are in the wrong relationship and keep trying to make it work?

How many people do you know who let their boss walk over them by, for example, phoning them while they're on holiday or generally stitching them up time after time? And what about the people who are constantly picked on and just keep taking it? And we all know at least someone who believes that they're not as lucky or as successful as other people. Or they believe that people they know just seem to sail through life – but can't work out why things don't work easily for them. That's the same sort of approach as being jealous of your friends who seem to be able to eat anything and still stay slim, or constantly asking yourself 'Why is it always me?'

If any of that chimes with anyone you know, here's what I would say to them if I knew them as well as you do. What you get in life is a direct result of what you do – consciously or unconsciously. If your autopilots are not getting you what you want out of your life, your work, or anything else, then all you need to do is change them.

Remember, your autopilots are all doing what they think is

best for you. Some of them are right about that and some of them are not. Remember Lisa who ended up with that autopilot that made her sick every time she got in the car (see pages 21–22)? That autopilot turned out to be a real dud but it meant well. So, in a very well-meaning way, it made her ill every time she got in the car in an attempt to stop her going to work.

Your autopilots are like well-meaning guard dogs. They guard you, they look after you and they care about your welfare. But sometimes they get it wrong and attack the postman thinking he's just as big a threat to you as a burglar. Lisa's autopilot, which tried to stop her from going to work, was simply trying to get her boss out of her life. It didn't think about the consequences of not turning up for work and it didn't explore the other possible ways of getting her boss out of her life. Autopilots are simple things.

So, what are you doing that's working? And what autopilots do you have that you might like to replace with better ones?

Obviously you've been learning new, successful autopilots to get what you want just by reading this book. That's been easy. Just by doing something differently – and repeatedly – is one way of chucking out a bad autopilot and replacing it with a good one. You find this in all the big rehab clinics around the world. Look at it like this: if you're an 'addict', all that really means is that you've got a bad autopilot. In rehab they get you to dismantle it slowly and gradually by changing everything that you do. They get you to brush your teeth with the other hand, perform your morning routine in a different order, hold your cutlery differently, break your contact with your regular world and so on. Basically they get you to do lots of things differently. That loosens the autopilot enough to allow you to replace it with a better one. And then you practise your new habit until it's second nature. The old one dies away as soon as you stop using it. All autopilots do that – good or bad. So – keep doing the stuff that works and stop doing the stuff that doesn't.

And if the process is enough to cure people of addiction to smack, crack, PCP, barbs, angel dust, tina, vodka, cigarettes, sex, video games and gambling, then what's left is pretty easy now, isn't it?

---

**DO THIS**

The fast autopilot replacement

1. Think of something that's not working for you – however big or small, it doesn't matter. It needs to be something that keeps cropping up or going wrong.

2. Think of what you'd be better off doing instead to put it right. Take your time. Don't move on until you have a proper answer.

3. Pick a time – the same time every day – to remind yourself of your new behaviour, using your internal dialogue. Repeat it to yourself over and over again at this time every day.

4. Do your new thing again and again. Start it now.

---

Bingo! New autopilot formed. Usually autopilots form naturally over a long period of time, without you having any control over them. You now know how to create the right autopilots quickly and deliberately.

You can do that whenever you want, with whatever you want. And the fact that you were able to answer steps 1 and 2 means you've already got a successful new autopilot. Here's a sneak preview of the sort of stuff that's in the 'Unmasked' section of this book later (see pages 243–249). By reading what we've been saying, you've built yourself a brand-new autopilot that gives you the ability to stop, look at what's around you and identify what you need to do differently if necessary. Now it's making sense to you consciously why we've been talking about mushrooms, sponges, Madonna, the English language, the person who got what he wanted at school but not after he left school, and my friend Mark with his shell necklace whose employers stopped supplying free mineral water. And that's a just few. Watch for the rest when you read this book for the second time. They're all the same story. The story is this: adapting quickly when things change gets you success. Staying the same does not get you what you want.

Without realizing it, you've been practising modern-day adaptability. And you can do it now. If you don't believe me, ask someone who hasn't been reading this book the first two questions in the fast autopilot replacement you've just done. Watch them struggle to think of what's not working or try to think of what they could do differently. Unless they're one of the few people who may have learned this autopilot naturally, they'll struggle much more than you. Because they don't have the autopilot that recognizes the need for adaptability.

Obviously, you now know what to do to make the techniques you've learned in this book second nature. Just keep doing them. Second nature means autopilot, by the way.

If you're going on holiday, on a break or just away from your daily routine in the near future, make a point of asking yourself the questions above again. Psychologically, that new autopilot of yours is even more effective when you've interrupted your pattern. Or to put it another way, your daily routine. If you're not going away, just choose another time when your pattern is interrupted. Like moving house, going back home, when you wake up in the middle of the night. Or when something happens out of your control, like if you split up with someone, you lose your job or you fall out with a close friend.

You only really needed one new autopilot, didn't you? The one that enables you to step back and identify bad autopilots so you can chuck them out and replace them with good ones.

# Here's the end again

Obviously you know all this already. Don't you?

- Some of what you want is in your own hands. A lot is in the hands of other people. This book is about how you get those things.

- In today's world, getting what you want means constantly adapting your behaviour to fit each situation.

- Thinking is made up of what you see, hear, feel and say to yourself inside your head. To get what you want, you need to ensure the other person is seeing, hearing, feeling and saying to themselves what you want them to.

- You have a specific set of principles, beliefs or values that are different from everyone else's. They are your codes and they determine how you think and behave. One of the obvious ways of not getting what you want is to assume that other people's codes are the same as yours.

- Getting what you want takes a bit of preparation and thought. Decide exactly what you want before you even begin to go about getting it.

- Everyone has been persuaded before. Most people can be persuaded again. Sometimes they can't be persuaded at all. But then there's always someone else you can persuade if that turns out to be the case.

- The best way to persuade somebody is through their unconscious, or subconscious.

- Sometimes you need to be on the same wavelength as the other person to get what you want. At other times you need to be on different wavelengths.

- To get what you want, you need to work out what the other person wants first.

- Playing the celebrity is the most effective way of getting what you want.

- Getting personal or getting impersonal can get you what you want too, depending on the situation.

- Everyone likes credit. Give people some – but not too much.

- People will often keep their word if you make them feel they owe you.

- The words you choose, and the way you say them, can persuade people without them realizing.

- Be ready for your enemies and be prepared to stop them getting what they want.

# Remember you need this book

You're in a room you've never been in before and it's one you've created. It's your room, your memory room. Your room is exactly how you want it to be. Some people have a small room, and some have a big room. The room is bright and vivid – full of colours you like. In the centre of the room is a table with a telephone on it. There are four large doors leading off the room. Each of the doors connects you to another room; the room you're in now is your connection room.

Door number 1 has a rolled-out red carpet leading to it and is boldly marked with the letters VIP. This door is for celebrities. You open the door and walk into the room. You see a mirror surrounded by light bulbs. The sort of mirror used by a film star in a dressing room.

Now turn around, to the table with the telephone. Go up to door number 2. It is shiny and metallic, the door to a lift. Push the button to call the lift. The door opens with a ping. On the inside of the lift are two shiny, chunky buttons. One button is clearly marked with the symbol of your gender, like you see on a WC. The other button is marked with the same symbol but it is crossed out in red. The first button takes you to the human floor and the second to the inhuman floor.

Go back to the room with the telephone and walk up to the third door. This is locked. There is no key and no keyhole. Instead, you have to swipe your card, like in some hotels. This door doesn't take an ordinary door card, it takes your credit card. To open the door, you need to give it some credit. Swipe your credit card to open the door. An alarm bell rings and at the same time a red light flashes above the door – you hear a computer voice say 'Warning, credit strictly limited'.

Go back into the connection room. There's one more door, the only door with a handle. The handle is massive and feels solid. To open the door, you have to put both hands on the handle and hold them to it.

Turn around again. You hadn't noticed until now but there's a button. A red button. It's encased in glass and there's a sign above it saying 'Press only in emergency, once you've tried everything'.

Once you've got to know your rooms really well, go back into each one and add some objects of your own that represent each technique in more detail. For example, you might want to put a surgeon's white coat in the celebrity room to represent expertise and authority. Or there might be no handle on the other side of the 'Hold them to it' door – meaning people won't be able to back out of the room once they've gone through and it's clicked shut behind them. Use your imagination now and do the rest. Do it your way.

# You need this book unmasked

This is the part where we play it straight. No fancy language patterns, no unconscious tricks, no accelerated learning, no embedding, no nothing. We're just telling you more about some of the unconscious stuff we've been using so you can get a deeper understanding of what you've been learning and how you've been learning it. Read this part of the book once you've got a proper grasp of the first part. After you understand this section too, you'll be brilliant. Think of it as the icing on the cake. This list is by no means exhaustive. We're giving you some examples of the main techniques we've used to 'persuade' your brain to learn more quickly.

Ready? Here we go. Starting from the beginning of the book:

### To start with, here's the end (see page vii)

We explained this a bit when we did it. It's based on a speed-reading technique that encourages your unconscious to start absorbing ideas before your conscious starts to process them. The fact that you're reading a list of principles that you haven't learned yet will get your brain working on them straight away. That means when you get to them in the body of the book, your brain is already familiar with them in headline form, and is able to process what you learn much more quickly and easily. Once you read the same points again in the middle of the book (we call it 'Here's the end again'), your brain recognizes what it's already picked up, prepares itself for what you're about to learn next and your learning is reinforced even further. By the time you get to this a third time – at the end of the book – the whole book is crystallized in headline form in your mind. And because you've seen it all before, you recognize it. This technique is great for whenever you want to learn something new.

### Introduction: Why you need this book to get what you want (see page xi)

A presupposition. The title of this chapter presupposes that you do need the book to get what you want. It gets your mind focusing on *why* you need it. This persuades your brain at an unconscious level that you will benefit from the book – and as a result it will retain as much of it as possible.

**Of course, it would be so much better if you could get people on your side instantly, wouldn't it (see page xi)**

Stating the obvious 'of course', persuades you how much better life's going to be once you can persuade people more effectively. And 'wouldn't it' is the question that's not a question. Note the absence of a question mark, so your internal dialogue – as you read it – has a downward intonation which acts as a command. You have absorbed – effortlessly – and unconsciously that getting people instantly on your side is a massive part of getting what you want.

**It's a formula, a template, a recipe, a simple process to get what you want (see page xiv)**

Inclusive language. Some people think more scientifically than others. At least one of these four words should strike a chord with pretty much everyone.

**By the way, this is probably a good time to clear something up. Some people might call this 'manipulation' (see page xiv)**

An inoculation. If you were likely to have concerns in the back of your mind (or in your rulebook) that this book was about how to be 'manipulative' in a negative way, that would have stood in the way of your acceptance of the principles, and would have impeded your learning. By inoculating – in other words, stating your concerns and clearing them up in advance – we help you to open your mind to the max so you can pick up as much as possible. It also makes sure your internal dialogue doesn't start saying the wrong things and get in the way of your progress.

### A lot of people who have experienced our live seminars have asked us to write this book (see page xvi)

We're using our celebrity to get you to keep reading and pay attention. The fact that we have done lots of live seminars about this makes you sit up and listen. Add to that the fact that other people were asking us to write the book, and you open your mind to what you're about to learn. If other people want this stuff, then it must be worth reading, mustn't it?

### That means you are now reading the book, following the words, and seeing a few things in your mind's eye . . . (see page xviii)

'That means' is a cause and effect statement. Creating a causal link between two ideas, whether that link really exists or not, gets your brain to accept the bit that comes after 'that means'. For example, if you fancy an ice cream, but you're with a friend on a diet, just say 'Look, the sun's come out for the first time in weeks – *that means* we're allowed an ice cream just for today.' So by saying 'That means you are now reading the book, following the words, and seeing a few things in your mind's eye', I am getting your unconscious agreement to do just that.

## And if you weren't seeing pictures in your mind's eye before . . . (see page xviii)

Another inoculation. If you disagreed with the earlier statement that you were looking at pictures in your mind's eye (because some people do that more readily than others), we have negated any possible weakening of rapport with you by accepting that you might not have done at that point. Even though . . .

## . . . you certainly are now, aren't you? (see page xviii)

Pacing your experience. A true statement of fact about what you are experiencing deepens rapport with you, gets your internal dialogue saying 'Yes', so you keep reading and become even more engaged.

## Making the right pictures in your head can be very useful (see page xviii)

People tend to be either motivated by 'pain' or 'gain'. Some people call it 'carrot' or 'stick'. We use two distinct motivational patterns here to ensure we motivate you.

## So, how are you? (see page xviii)

The use of the word 'you' engages you deeply and is in the form of a question to activate your internal dialogue. You feel obliged to answer the question internally to yourself. This deepens rapport. When you're talking to people, they'll warm to you much more quickly if you keep using the word 'you' (i.e. talking about *them*) rather than the word 'I' (which would be talking about *yourself*).

### Right, we need to talk about your parents having sex (see page 1)

A pattern interruption. There you were just getting used to the tone, style and nature of the book. Your unconscious was starting to come up with a general idea of what to expect, and suddenly – your parents are having sex. What's that got to do with what you'd been reading before? Interrupting your pattern every so often ensures you keep giving the book your maximum attention so you retain as much as you can. Pattern interruptions are a good way of breaking connection if you want to buy yourself time, or grab someone's attention again if they're drifting off.

### Mark with the shell necklace, the other Mark, his wife and the estate agent, Herc the hamster, the man with the hi-visibility jacket, Sharon and so on.

Storytelling. You've read a lot of stories in this book. Storytelling is one of the best methods for influence. It's how you can get your points across most effectively. Stories create pictures, sounds and emotions in your mind as you follow them. And you take on the point of each story at an unconscious level. When persuading people, tell as many stories as you can. And, in case you're wondering, every story in this book is true.

Now keep reading the rest of the book *again* and see how many more examples you can spot and that you haven't got yet. By the way, the previous sentence *did* contain at least three language patterns. Can you spot them?

# Pocket reference

Obviously, there are lots of ways of getting what you want. There's no set formula for a particular scenario, but here are some suggested techniques, or combinations of techniques, to get what you want in certain situations. If you're not successful at first, try something else. You're adaptable.

## At work

### Be the boss when you're not really the boss

'Use your celebrity' (see chapter 12), 'Give them *some* credit' (see chapter 4), 'Get connection' (see chapter 9) and then break connection (see chapter 15), get connection and then break connection . . .

## Get out of staying late but keep the boss happy

Use 'Yes means no' (see page 123) and be human (see chapter 13). And then 'Hold them to it' (see chapter 16).

## Stand out among colleagues in the eyes of your boss

Use any of the language devices in Chapter 11.

## Get a promotion or pay rise

Be hugely human (see chapter 13) when you talk about yourself and why you need the promotion. Say 'I shouldn't really tell you this but . . .' and explain how important the money is to you and why. Then be inhuman and talk about how much the company will benefit from you being in this new position. Once you get an agreement in principle, even a slight agreement, say 'Don't say "yes" unless you mean it'. Allow them to repeat their agreement. Later, use 'Hold them to it' (see chapter 16).

## Shaft a colleague who's trying to shaft you

Press the 'Red Button' (see page 216).

## At a job interview

Get connection and keep connection (see chapter 9). Ask the 'ideal question' (see page 119) – 'tell me about your ideal candidate for this job' – and then make sure all your answers fit the bill. Use their very words, don't paraphrase. When you want to make a point about yourself, use 'It's not important, but it is really' (see page 123) to get it under the radar.

### Get what you want out of a meeting

Do 'The meeting before the meeting' (see page 124), then 'Give them *some* credit' (see chapter 14), and then 'Hold them to it' (see chapter 16). The ideal question (see page 119) can work magic in meetings, and get them saying yes (see page 116).

## Outside of work

### Get your partner to put down the remote

Use 'A polite way to say "Shut up and listen to me"' (see page 123).

### Get your partner to leave you alone so you can watch TV

'Break connection' (see chapter 15), offer to switch it off and watch it later using 'Yes means no' (see page 123).

### Served at the bar

'Get connection' (see chapter 9), or 'use your celebrity' (see chapter 12).

### Get out of a parking fine

Be precise about who you need to influence first and human-ize like hell (see chapter 13). Most people try to get out of a ticket by trying to influence the traffic warden there and then. This rarely works because the traffic warden has already decided to give you a ticket. Much better is a formal appeal afterwards. Before you appeal, strike first with a very human letter of complaint to the authorities. 'Paint your own pain', graphically. Give them a sob story, make your case emotional. Mention your health, a sick relative – anything. And paint the traffic warden as having been heartless and unreasonable for giving you the ticket

### Carry out building work without annoying the neighbours

Strike first with a handwritten note to your neighbours thanking them in advance for their understanding. Explain that work will be taking place. Accompany the note with a small gift – chocolates or something, 'Go over and above' (see pages 203–207) in advance.

### Deal with noisy neighbours

Get connection (see chapter 9) and humanize first (see chapter 13). Explain the impact it's having, face to face. Use 'State the obvious' (see page 115) and say something like 'I know I don't need to tell you how loud your music was last night' . . .

'Obviously I'm asking you to keep it down in future.' Smile if you can. Lay it on thick. If that doesn't work, suddenly go very inhuman and get someone to 'Use their celebrity' (see chapter 12) to contact them in writing on your behalf (e.g. a lawyer). Mention the legal options that you have.

### Deal with bossy friends

Use 'Give them *some* credit' (see chapter 14), and 'A polite way to say "Shut up and listen to me"' (see page 123). Get out of obeying their orders by using 'Yes means no' (see page 123).

### Go where you want to go (holiday/bar/restaurant)

Use 'Do it without quotes' (see pages 122–123) and 'Command and command' (see page 118). For example, 'I've read brilliant things about Pizza Hut. Let's eat there and then go clubbing somewhere.' Give any other rival ideas *some* credit (see chapter 14).

### Spot a liar

Know your enemy (see chapter 17).

### Get people to like you – first time, every time

'Get connection' (see chapter 9), listen to specific words/language/vocabulary that they use and use the *very same* words throughout the conversation. Focus on keeping connection all the way through, use 'The question that's not really a question' (see pages 115–116) and 'I shouldn't really tell you this but . . .' (see page 118).

## Get a seat on a crowded train

First do a Meryl (see pages 94–96). Think of a time when you've felt genuinely confident. Remember the pictures, the sounds and use your internal dialogue (see pages 19–23) to tell yourself how confident that makes you feel. Walk straight up to someone – make sure it's a man – and tell him you really need the seat *because* . . . and give a reason. Any reason. It could be that you're feeling really tired, ill, or that you have something important you need to read. The fact that you've said 'because . . .' will usually get you the seat. This sounds much more daunting than it is. And once you've done it once, you'll want to do it again and again. Go on, do it once!

## Attract the person you really want to talk to without offending the rest of their group.

'Get connection' (see chapter 9) from a distance. Once you've got it, break it (see chapter 15). Then get it again.

## Get rid of someone you get stuck with at a party

Set a time constraint using 'This or that' (see page 117). For example, 'I'm not sure if my cab is coming at eleven or quarter past.' 'I'm not sure if my mates are leaving at eleven or quarter past.' Gradually 'Break connection' (see chapter 15) from that moment on.

### Get your child to do as he or she is told

Ask 'Would you do me a favour?' Wait for the answer 'Yes'. Then ask them to do what you want them to do. And 'Hold them to it' (see chapter 16).

### How to get chatted up

'Get connection' (see chapter 9) then 'Break connection' (see chapter 15). Do that a few times in a row. Then get connection again. And wait. Or 'Use your celebrity' (see chapter 12).

### Make sure a promise is kept

Use 'Hold them to it' (see chapter 16).

### Get an extension on paying bills

Be human (see chapter 13), use 'I shouldn't really tell you this but . . .' (see page 118) and give what seems to be a very personal reason for having financial problems. You can also blend 'State the obvious' (see page 115) with 'Leaps of logic' (see pages 117–118). For example, explain why you're short of money and say 'Obviously that means I can't pay until . . .'

## Second-guess other people

Get inside their head (see chapter 7).

## Get away with a minor road offence

Depends on the police officer! Maximize your chances by being very human (see chapter 13). Admit to your guilt and then say 'but' (see page 118) – and follow it with 'I shouldn't really tell you this but . . .' (see page 118) and give a really good human reason for what you've done. For example, 'I know I'm in the wrong, I know it's a one-way street but – and I shouldn't really tell you this – I've just split up with someone and I just don't know what I'm doing at the moment.' If you're a woman, the odd tear wouldn't go amiss here. It works even better if you're a man.

## Get a refund

Be human (see chapter 13). 'Give them *some* credit' (see chapter 14). Use 'Leaps of logic' (see pages 117–118), to explain why you must have the money back. For example: 'I love coming to this shop. It's one of my favourites.' 'I know you pride yourself on your customer service. That must mean you're willing to make an exception in my case.' If you can, mention the name of a shop assistant who usually serves you.

## Quickly exit a busy train onto a crowded platform

'Use your celebrity' (see chapter 12). Just after the doors open, pause and watch the crowd part in front of you.

### Jump the queue

Be confident. Walk to the person at the front of the queue and ask to go ahead. Say 'because' . . . and give a reason. Any reason really, as long as it sounds sensible. The word 'because' does all the work for you. Once you get permission, thank the person profusely – and the people behind them – holding your hand up if you can.

### Get out of trouble with someone who's annoyed with you

Ask 'The ideal question' (see page 119). 'What do I need to do ideally to make it up to you/put things right?'

### Cancel an arrangement at the last minute and get away with it

Be inhuman (see chapter 13). Text at the last minute – say something urgent has come up and you'll call them tomorrow to explain. Say you're really sorry, in the text. Call the next day and give a good reason. They can't be too angry with you because you've said sorry and you're explaining *after* the event. The inconvenience to them has passed – and they can't talk you into changing your mind.

### Make a purchase your local convenience store, when you've forgotten your wallet

Pick up the things you want to buy and take them to the cash register. Reach for your wallet, turn to the shop assistant, apologize and be very human (see chapter 13). 'State the obvious' (see page 115), and say 'As you know, I come in here all the time' and tell them how you live close by. 'Give them *some* credit' (see chapter 14) – for being so handy and convenient and then do 'This or that' (see page 117): say that since they have such long opening hours, you can either pay them first thing in the morning on your way out, or at the end of the day on your way home. Ask which they would prefer.

## Get your partner to take a serious conversation seriously

If you've had deep and meaningful talks, but you worry your partner is just going to revert to old ways straight away – you need to 'Hold them to it' (see chapter 16). But before that, you need to go inhuman (see chapter 13). Yes, inhuman. Write an email to your partner, summing up what you discussed – and saying what you want to happen as a result (not what you don't want – remember!). Using 'A polite way to say "shut up and listen to me"' (see page 123) works well in this context. So do 'It's not important, but it is really' (see page 123), and to get proper commitment 'Don't say "yes" unless you mean it' (see pages 121–122).

## Get your partner to stop doing something else and pay attention to you

Be human (see chapter 13) and use 'It's not important, but it is really' (see page 123).

### Impress the parents

Make them the most important people you need to influence; first 'Give them *some* credit' (see chapter 14). Be human (see chapter 13).

### Use someone's toilet when you're caught short

Walk into a bar, restaurant or hotel suitable for the way you're dressed, chatting to an imaginary person on your mobile phone. Walk straight to the WC. In the unlikely event that a member of staff apprehends you, just hold up your hand, point to your phone, and mouth 'Sorry'. Then hold up your index finger as if to say 'Talk to you in a minute'. Make sure you keep walking as you do it – don't stop. Once you've been, you've been!

### Get the day off

If your boss recognizes you have celebrity (see chapter 12), use it. If not, get connection (see chapter 9) and be human (see chapter 13). Give a good, human reason why you need the day off, and strike first with something you can do for your boss in return for them being flexible – but say it in a 'Yes means no' (see page 123) kind of way so you probably won't end up having to do it. In most cases, it's important that this is at least seen as an offer of an exchange and not a favour.

## Get back with the ex

'Use your celebrity' (see chapter 12). Once you're about to get back together, use 'Don't say "yes" unless you mean it' (see pages 121–122). And 'Hold them to it' (see chapter 16).

## Get a loan/credit

Be human (see chapter 13) – get face to face with a bank manager or account manager if you can. Explain why you need credit in a really human way. Say that you know it's usually decided by computer on a points system, and ask how they can help you if the computer says no. Use 'It's not important, but it is really' (see page 123), and 'I shouldn't really tell you this but . . .' (see page 118). When you get really good, use 'Leaps of logic' (see pages 117–118) and get them saying yes (see page 116).

# Acknowledgements

Our publisher, Simon & Schuster, particularly Kerri Sharp, for its professionalism and enthusiasm – and helping us make the transition from presenters to authors.

Our book agent, Antony Topping, for keeping our expectations under control.

Our management agent, Sue Ayton, for helping us to create those expectations in the first place.

Ski, for making sure we got it finished on time.

Richard, for his legendary eye for detail.

And the many people we have encountered for providing us with the stories in this book.

# Outer boroughs

- HAVERING
- REDBRIDGE
- WALTHAM FOREST

___

out of London

West of London